THE JACKIE ROBINSON STORY

Robinson played both offense and defense for the UCLA Bruins.

"If Jackie hadn't played football he might have been the greatest of all basketball players."

Then he journeyed to the NCAA championship at Minneapolis and broadjumped 25 feet again.

The spotlight was on Robinson as the first Negro to play in a World Series.

THE Jackie Robinson STORY

By ARTHUR MANN

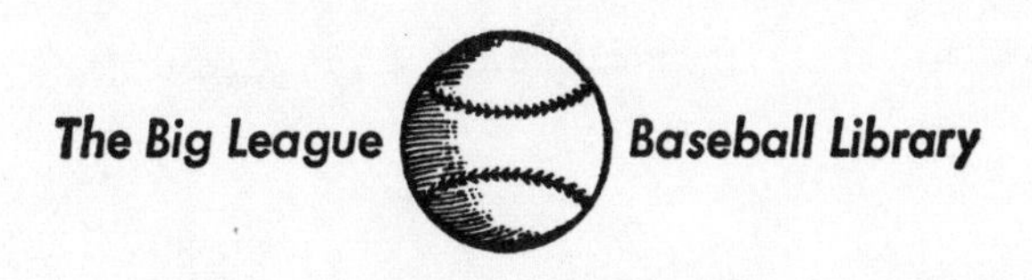

GROSSET & DUNLAP

Publishers • NEW YORK

Printed in the United States of America

FOREWORD

Millions of people have watched Jackie Robinson play baseball. But what those millions have seen on the baseball field was only the last stage in the intriguing and complex development of a great athlete. This book tells the inspiring story of that development.

Arthur Mann, co-author of the Jackie Robinson movie, is uniquely well qualified to write this important book. Not only was he the sensitive and inquisitive reporter who followed Robinson's career even before his entrance into organized baseball; but, because of his human qualities as well as his professional qualifications, Arthur Mann was hired by Branch Rickey, Manager of the Dodgers, as his assistant in recruiting team members. In that capacity, Mann was personally involved in the series of events which led up to the historic integration of the first Negro into baseball.

That is not to say that Rickey undertook a campaign especially pointed at integrating baseball. Rickey had only one drive: the pursuit of players who could bring a pennant to Brooklyn. Whatever other characteristics these players had mattered little. What counted was, "Can he play ball?"

Up to the day when Jackie Robinson's name appeared on the line-up card of a major league baseball team, organized baseball had not covered itself with glory in the matter of fair employment practices. Until that time, no one had ever stopped to consider whether a Negro aspirant to a team had talent on the baseball field. He was neatly excluded from competition and was neither encouraged nor permitted to rise to the eminence of the Big Leagues. Yet, in fairness, it must be stated that the inherently democratic character of the game of baseball (as opposed to the autocratic character of the *business* of baseball) unlocked the door to the future of the Negro in America's national sport.

The checks and balances of skill, strategy and power on the ball field, regarded in the proper perspective, cannot be influenced by race, creed or color. Baseball's basic rules of procedure are above such limitations. Victory can come only as the result of a communal effort by nine variously skilled individuals. Yet, as in all democratic organizations, opportunities for outstanding individual performances are present whenever baseball is played.

Jackie Robinson's willingness and ability to do just that: to take chances and grasp opportunities, were what caused him to shine on the diamond and in the memory of his fans. For Robinson's native skills, although adequate, were not the stuff of which diamond immortals are cut. But these skills, in combination with his highly developed aptitude for taking advantage of every opportunity that came his way on the field, put Jackie right up there with the other all-time greats of baseball history.

Once, in a game against the Dodgers' fiercest rivals, the Giants, Robinson, still in his prime, proved his value to his team and his appeal with the crowd with a dazzling show of opportunism. What he did was uncomplicated and it was beautiful.

The Dodgers were behind. One could sense their frustration in the tense way they were playing. One could tell, at least a real Dodger fan could tell, that it was a losing day. Then Robinson managed to make it to third base, only ninety feet away from home.

He began his tantalizing dance. The lefty Giant pitcher looked over his shoulder and back at the batter. Then he looked at Robinson. Jack was taunting him. Try as he would, the lefty couldn't keep Robinson close enough to third. As he slowly wound up for his pitch, Robinson tore halfway home. Then, completely confident and defiant, he raced back to third. This game went on for fully five minutes. There was little action on the field. The pitcher had managed to throw only three pitches in those five minutes. There was bedlam in the stands. Everyone, including the pitcher, knew what Jackie would do if he could force the chance.

He finally did it! He tore in for the plate like an express train. The pitcher, by this time emotionally exhausted, was too limp to bother with even token resistance. He never made the challenging throw home. As Robinson ploughed into the plate with what turned out to be an unnecessary slide, the pitcher took the ball and his glove, threw them both high in the air over his head and, letting them drop behind him, walked off the mound straight to the peace of an early and soothing shower. There was not a fan in the ballpark, regardless of persuasion, who did not rise at that moment to pay deafening tribute to the daring player who, by guts alone, singlehandedly, had turned the tide in his team's favor.

Even at the advanced (for baseball) age of 36, Robinson electrified a crowded Yankee Stadium during the 1955 World Series, by creating another opportunity when his team needed one badly. The Dodgers were three runs in the hole and there was one out in the eighth inning. Then Robby hit an 0–2 "waste" pitch hard at the third baseman. The ball ricocheted off the fielder's glove and Robby kept going on to second while the runner ahead of him advanced to third. A long fly advanced both runners.

Now, once again, Robinson stood at third base. He began his exasperating sprints up and down the line, measuring the opposing pitcher, annoying him and preparing for the pay-off. This time the pitcher was the redoubtable Whitey Ford, a foe to be contended with in such an encounter. But Robby found that precious instant of advantage only he could have seen, and on his fourth try he stole home on a hair's-breadth play.

Though the Dodgers dropped that game 6–5, they finally captured the Series from the Yankees. Robinson wasn't the only hero of the triumph. Nevertheless, his spirit was undeniably a Dodger strong point.

His unquenchable spirit for the game, for the competition, combined with the untiring efforts of many people, make up the Jackie Robinson success story. Not the least of these great efforts on Robinson's behalf was put forward by Arthur Mann: friend, counselor and chronicler to the first Negro to enter the Major Leagues; the first Negro to be enshrined in the Baseball Hall of Fame.

CHAPTER 1

IT WAS early 1943 and Branch Rickey was beginning a five-year contract as general manager of the Brooklyn Dodgers. He had left St. Louis where for thirty years he had been a builder of baseball—five years with the American League Browns and a quarter-century with the National League Cardinals. He had built the Cardinals from a shoestring to a property worth more than three million dollars. But no Negro had ever been sold a grandstand ticket in St. Louis.

Now he was presenting a startling program to the stockholders and Board of Directors of the Brooklyn Club in one of his earliest meetings with them. They knew him as a man of ideas and energy, for that was why they had coaxed him from the mid-West. And he didn't disappoint. Within a few minutes he had launched into a plan that was to lead the Dodgers eventually to a dominating position in organized baseball, even while the nation was at war.

"Major league clubs are dismissing scouts and their

bird dog helpers in wholesale fashion," Rickey said, and paused to flick some cigar ashes into a tray. "That is sound business under the circumstances, and they cannot be criticized for it. But I have a different theory about scouting in our current wartime situation.

"It is based upon the inherent impatience of our soldiers. I saw it in France during World War One. Somehow, when our boys get on foreign land for purposes of fighting, they either become impatient, homesick or just plain ornery. Regardless of the exact reason, they have the happy faculty of ending foreign wars with delightful speed. And I would not be surprised if the same held true for the American boys on foreign soil now. In fact, I'm rather counting on it.

"On the very strength of this analysis, I would like to offer a plan that has a good chance of unprecedented success in baseball . . . and an equal chance of colossal failure—by colossal, I mean in terms of money loss, which will be one hundred percent, if the plan fails."

Once again there was a pause as ashes were carefully separated from the glowing end of the cigar. All eyes in the room followed this movement while waiting for an explanation to the cryptic plan. There was no looking behind the deepset eyes, hidden in the shadows of shaggy brows and behind highlighted spectacles.

"Instead of dismissing our scouts and their affiliated bird dogs," Rickey continued, and scanned the faces of his audience, "I would hire all the capable scouts I could find, up to a certain point, of course. Rather than minimize activities in the field, I would increase them; enlarge their scope until our scouts are contacting every available baseball prospect down through age sixteen—yes, even fifteen, if possible."

"Would you sign these boys?" he was asked.

Rickey's heavy brown hair tumbled over his forehead as he nodded vigorously.

"Yes, sir!" he declared. "And if the war continues well past the two-and-a-half-year mark, this man-power will be absorbed by the military, as well it should be. We will lose everything, which would mean an investment of a hundred thousand dollars, a sum which this organization can ill afford to lose."

The listeners shifted uneasily. It was a tremendous amount in wartime, not knowing for sure whether the full schedule would be permitted by Washington. They recalled that the 1918 season had been curtailed by World War I.

"On the other hand, gentlemen," Rickey continued, and the suggestion of a smile softened his leonine features, "the war *could* end within two or two and a half years. I have a strong hunch, based on my own experience and faith in our soldiers: that it will not go much beyond the two-year mark. If so, the Brooklyn Baseball Club will possess so large a complement of youth—boys of all skills and sizes—that our position for the future will be assured. By moving fast and carefully, we could be in an enviable position."

He tossed the half-smoked cigar into the wastebasket in a gesture of finality, and looked from one to the other.

"But I will not make this decision alone," he said. "I

need your wholehearted support. Remember what the program may cost. Remember that every penny of the investment may be lost. On the other hand, realize that we could wind up with more ball players than any other club in baseball history has possessed. Gentlemen, it's up to you!"

The factors of the program were discussed at length. There was no question about its merit. But it was also daring, almost brazen, because the Brooklyn Baseball Club at the time was considerably in debt; not as much, however, as it once had been. Five years of the Larry MacPhail firecracker regime had produced more than noise. The ebullient redhead had brought prosperity to Brooklyn and had reduced indebtedness considerably, but he had not been able to construct more than a one-season winner. He was a team-maker, but not a team-builder. The Rickey plan was for the long haul. Still, it was a tremendous gamble with non-existent funds.

Or was it? How can you say that betting on the nation's fighting forces is a gamble? Wasn't everybody betting on those same soldiers, sailors and marines? Weren't our whole economy, our government, our businesses, our homes and churches "gambling" on these boys?

Rickey was rewarded with a full vote of confidence in the proposed program. He was given a go-ahead signal, a green light all the way. And immediately he set in motion one of the most comprehensive schemes of bush-beating for players that baseball has ever known. Backed by sufficient funds, he was further aided by thirty years of scouting background in St. Louis. He knew the best talent hunters. Some of them had recently lost jobs. Release of scouts by other clubs gave him the pick of the field.

Several times during the meeting, Rickey had been tempted to reveal a long and closely guarded desire in his scheme of baseball things. But he fought off temptation with the conclusion that it would be better to take the matter up individually with members of the board and stockholders.

It was George McLaughlin, president of the Brooklyn Trust Company, whom Rickey first approached. McLaughlin was neither board member nor stockholder, but his bank had long been the financial backlog and bulwark of the Brooklyn Club in days of heavy credit financing of Dodger doings and dealings. He was consulted not only as a banker, but as a former New York City Police Commissioner, a civic leader and a man with a deep knowledge and appreciation of social affairs. Rickey confided to McLaughlin that the scouting program just approved was an all-embracing one, and would be all that the term implied.

"We are going to beat the bushes, and we will take whatever comes out," Rickey said with a twinkle in his gray-blue eyes. "And that might include a Negro player or two."

The banker eyed the baseball man for an instant and then emitted a characteristic grunt.

"I don't see why not," he said. "You *might* come up with something."

Within a short while Rickey had tested the various stockholders and Board members of the Dodgers individually on his over-all intentions. His approach was casual, almost subtle, for he wanted to frighten nobody. His idea was to have it a natural transition of thinking before it became a reality. He offered no details or predictions.

By clearing with his sponsors, Rickey completed the first step in a carefully drawn program of procedure to locate and weigh the possibilities of Negro baseball players. This program consisted of a half-dozen different steps or hurdles, each of which had to be cleared without accident or fault in order for the project to succeed. The plan had six stages, as follows:

1. The backing and sympathy of the Dodgers' directors and stockholders, whose investment and civic standing had to be considered and protected.
2. Picking a Negro who would be the right man on the field.
3. Picking a Negro who would also be the right man off the field.
4. A good reaction from the press and public.
5. Backing and thorough understanding from the Negro race, to avoid misinterpretation and abuse of the project.
6. Acceptance of the player by his teammates.

As he incorporated the project into his ambitious scouting plans, Branch Rickey felt that he could clear the first five conditions before bringing a Negro into the big leagues. He readily admitted that the sixth condition could not be tackled until all other conditions had been satisfied and the player was a member of the Dodgers, or about to become one. At no time did he forget that sectionalism among baseball players might be strong enough to outweigh all other factors. That it would outweigh them, he always doubted.

Despite hue and cry to the contrary, this was not a long-range sociological scheme. The social aspects were entirely secondary. The motivating force was and always had been to locate better baseball players. The essence of Rickey's baseball philosophy is to win.

Understandably Rickey was conscious of the sociological importance of the move. He knew perfectly well what the finding and hiring of a Negro baseball player or players would symbolize. But he had watched them come to the front in boxing to succeed in that sport in virtually all divisions of weight. He had seen them express themselves physically in track and field competition to a point where they dominated the first place situation in the Olympic Games at Berlin, Germany, in 1936. He did not expect domination by Negroes in baseball, nor does he expect it today. He simply felt that, if they could be great athletes in one or two sports, they could be great athletes in a third sport. And why not baseball?

He was further encouraged by the fact that wartime baseball was at a low point of skill, perhaps as low as it ever had been. But the fans couldn't appreciate the lower caliber of baseball skill, because it was general, and competition was just as keen as before.

It was possible that this over-all condition of lowered

skill might continue through a definite post-war period of perhaps five years. Even if Negro baseball players were not up to big league or top minor league skill on the basis of normal standards, the best could certainly satisfy wartime demands. Competitive spirit and high physical skill and aptitudes might make them better.

What with reorganizing the Brooklyn Dodger team that had blown the 1942 pennant, and acclimating his personal and business life to a new organization after twenty-five years with the St. Louis Cardinals, the actual search for Negro players was not of major significance in 1943. Rickey assembled a scouting staff with great care and the scouts were equally careful in contacting their bird dogs. It is a fact, however, that he actually had reports on players in Puerto Rico as well as Cuba before the end of 1943. These came from confidential Latin emissaries, and even from a university professor, a personal friend, who happened to be making a Caribbean tour. By the middle of 1944 Rickey had a fair idea of what Negro talent was available in all the Caribbean countries, Central and South America and Mexico. He was now scrutinizing the so-called Negro leagues in the United States.

Rickey regarded it as an indictment of himself and of baseball to acknowledge the existence of a so-called Negro league, just as he would be if obliged to designate a Catholic or Protestant lineup, or a Jewish and Christian outfield. To a writer who questioned him pointedly on the written reference to baseball as a "national white pastime" instead of merely the national pastime, Rickey acknowledged that, if there were such a thing as Negro baseball *per se*, then most certainly organized baseball should be designated as *white* baseball, inasmuch as it contained no Negroes, and particularly since the Negro players had to be characterized in their league in order to be identified properly.

As a result of this constant analysis, Rickey was thrown into a thorough study of so-called Negro baseball. It did not take him long to conclude that they were not leagues in the accepted sense of the word. He learned that the so-called league schedule was, in fact, a front for a monopolistic game-booking business, controlled by booking agents in Chicago, Philadelphia and New York.

He learned that the teams of the leagues played an inconsistent number of ball games in league competition; that the team with the better roster would play between 40 and 45 games a year, while the poor team, a correspondingly poor attraction, would play as few as 25 or 30 league games. Yet, the Negro teams in this league played as many as ten and twelve exhibition games each week. They were known to play as many as three games in a single day, sometimes playing the same team twice daily in different localities.

This was a barnstorming type of baseball, and perfectly acceptable as such. What he objected to was the word "league" to confuse the public into believing that the operation was similar to that of organized baseball. One look at a five-week schedule, taken at random, illustrates the casual character of the competition. From April 29 to May 31, inclusive, here is a record of games played among the teams of the Negro National League:

HOMESTEAD GRAYS:
Baltimore Elite Giants, 6; New York Black Yankees, 6; Philadelphia Stars, 7; New York Cubans, 3; Newark Eagles, 1. Total: 23.

BALTIMORE ELITE GIANTS:
Homestead Grays, 6; New York Cubans, 6; Newark Eagles, 4; Philadelphia Stars, 3; New York Black Yankees, 2. Total: 21.

NEW YORK CUBANS:
Baltimore Elite Giants, 6; Philadelphia Stars, 4; Newark Eagles, 4; Homestead Grays, 3; New York Black Yankees, 2. Total: 19.

NEW YORK BLACK YANKEES:
Homestead Grays, 6; Newark Eagles, 5; Philadelphia Stars, 3; Baltimore Elite Giants, 3; New York Cubans, 2. Total: 18.

PHILADELPHIA STARS:
Homestead Grays, 7; New York Cubans, 4; Newark Eagles, 4; Baltimore Elite Giants, 3; New York Black Yankees, 3. Total: 21.

NEWARK EAGLES:
New York Black Yankees, 5; Baltimore Elite Giants, 4; New York Cubans, 4; Philadelphia Stars, 4; Homestead Grays, 1. Total: 18.

Significant in this sample 33-day schedule, is that the Homestead Grays and the Newark Eagles met only once, on a Sunday in Newark. Further revealing is the fact that the Homestead Grays met the Philadelphia Stars for the first time on the twenty-third day of this particular segment of the schedule, and then played their seven games in seven days!

They were hampered, of course, by the vagaries in the team schedules of organized baseball whose parks they used. Of the above seven games between the Homestead Grays and Philadelphia Stars, six were played in Forbes Field, Pittsburgh, home of the Pirates, and the seventh game at Griffith Stadium, Washington, D. C. Significant is that none was played in Philadelphia, home of the Stars.

Rickey further learned that the Negro leagues did not have uniform player contracts, and few contracts, at all, except for crowd-pleasing stars like Satchel Paige, Josh Gibson and other celebrated figures whose box-office value put their incomes into the upper brackets. He learned that players were prevented from jumping from one team to another by the simple expedient of a gentleman's agreement, whereby the appearance of a player's name in the box score identified him as the property of that team, and untouchable.

Yet, these leagues issued averages for batting and pitching and club standings, and they were offered to the public through newspapers much in the manner of the carefully compiled and authenticated statistics of organized baseball.

He found a decided lack of individual security, and such a complete absence of bargaining rights for the player that the situation amounted to a racket. Many big league baseball clubs were willing participants and beneficiaries, inasmuch as they rented their baseball parks to these booking agents for big Negro games at a guaranteed minimum of $1000 per game against 25% of the gross receipts. Since the booking agents exacted an additional 15% off the top, the Negro teams were left to survive on 60% of the gross receipts from which they paid taxes, salaries, maintenance, traveling fees, etc.

Little wonder that the teams engaged in a fabulous series of exhibition games between "league contests." It was necessary to maintain income from this type of baseball in order to survive.

Despite the unattractive and futureless field, young Negro players were being developed somewhere, and were somehow drifting into this unhealthy situation. Rickey interpreted this as a tribute to baseball itself, and the hold which the game has on youngsters of all ages and color. Baseball made them brothers under the skin, regardless of skin pigmentation. A black boy could sleep with his glove under his pillow so he could waken and smell the leather, the same as a white boy, Rickey concluded. In this respect, baseball was a common denominator second to none.

CHAPTER 2

NOT EVEN Branch Rickey's trusted scouts suspected his ulterior motive, and they were further thrown off the track in 1945 when, after the German surrender, he spearheaded a move to form what was called the United States League, a Negro organization with plans for baseball teams in key cities, one of which was Brooklyn. For himself, or for the Ebbets Field owners, he reserved a franchise and planned to organize the Brooklyn Brown Dodgers.

The founders of the United States League held their first meeting at the Theresa Hotel in Harlem, New York City, and were not only encouraged in the undertaking, but were loaned money to get the difficult situation started. In sharp contrast to inferior conditions elsewhere in Negro baseball, the United States League laid the groundwork for uniform player contracts, an equal schedule for all teams, a reserve clause for the retention of a player's services, a corresponding protection for the player himself in the form of salary guarantees, bargaining rights, transportation to and from training camp, skilled medical care, etc.

The United States League was a most ambitious undertaking, perhaps too big for the time it was attempted. Nor did it eliminate the "color" designation of a baseball player. But its primary purpose was to correct an evil that was black-eyeing baseball, and would serve as a stepping stone in the right direction.

Happily, it also served as an instrument to cloak Rickey's activity in the field of scouting Negro players. Three of his most trusted scouts, George Sisler, Wid Matthews and Clyde Sukeforth, turned in many reports on the colored candidates, but with the understanding and assumption that they were scouting for the Brown Dodgers.

Major league club owners were most conscious of the Negro situation and proposed to do something about it at a special meeting, held at Cleveland in the Spring of 1945, the gathering which also produced the election of Senator Albert B. Chandler to the post of Commissioner of Baseball. In a joint meeting of the American and National Leagues a four-man board was proposed to make a thorough study and prepare a report. Larry MacPhail, new president and part owner of the New York Yankees, was selected by the American League. Branch Rickey was named by the National.

They were to choose by mutual agreement two outstanding Negro figures to collaborate on the study and report. But it was Rickey's hope that Mordecai Johnson, president of Howard University, would be one Negro and a New York judge, perhaps Myles A. Paige, the other. This four-man board, however, was not given any power to act. At no time during the discussion of the Negro problem within the joint meeting did baseball indicate an intention or even a willingness to alter the tint of the color line. The four-man board was simply a panel to study, return a report to their league heads and perhaps offer a suggestion or two.

But the German armistice had thrown everybody into a dither. First, Branch Rickey had won his gamble, or a major point of it. The American soldiers had come pretty close to winning the war on foreign soil within the period expressed by Rickey's hunch. The war was not over, but the rest of it was only a matter of months.

Secondly, the cessation of European hostilities had made an alarming number of people eager to get on the band wagon for the correction of the world's injustices in wholesale fashion.

Thirdly, Rickey's bush-beating scouts were turning in a surprising number of Negro candidates for tryouts, along with the largest number of white high school baseball prodigies ever corralled under the jurisdiction of a single club. The cartoonists and jokesters lampooned Rickey's efforts in this field, referring to him as the Old Woman of the Shoe, Mother Rickey's Chickens, and so on.

Players as young as sixteen, yes fifteen, were lined up for activity in the uniforms of Brooklyn and a rapidly-growing minor-league farm system. The number of minor leagues had dropped to nine during the war. Now they were returning to activity and, as fast as they were re-formed, Brooklyn obtained an ownership franchise or a working agreement with an owner. He had the green personnel to supply the teams, and no one else did. The Brooklyn minor league teams eventually numbered twenty-seven and Rickey's prediction of "our position for the future will be assured" had come true.

Not only that, but Sisler, Matthews and Sukeforth were really excited over what they had seen while scouting the colored baseball teams of this country. Considerable talent was to be found in all sections.

At the same time people were becoming Negro-conscious throughout the nation, particularly among the politicians. It was reflected nationally in the Fair Employment Practice Committee, a body created by Executive Order 8802 in June, 1941, when A. Philip Randolph, president of the Brotherhood of Sleeping Car Porters, threatened to visit his union membership on President Roosevelt as a protest against Negroes being denied work in war factories. The non-discriminating clause was put into all war contracts and halted the march. At the war's end a move was made to inculcate this practice into general business throughout the nation to forestall Negro unemployment.

New York State expressed itself in behalf of the Negro through the Ives-Quinn Law, a non-discrimination project sponsored by Governor Dewey, and a committee appointed to see that it worked.

In New York City, Mayor LaGuardia formed the Anti-Discrimination Committee to relieve racial intolerance. Councilman Ben Davis, one of the eleven communists recently sentenced by Judge Medina, was up for re-election in mid-1945 and made a special appeal to the sports-minded voters. He issued a lurid but effective pamphlet showing two Negroes on the cover. One was a dead soldier lying in the leaves, obviously in Europe; the other pictured figure was a Negro baseball player. The caption read, "Good enough to die for his country, but not good enough for organized baseball!"

Mayor LaGuardia made a special appeal to baseball leaders when he asked that the Rickey-MacPhail four-man committee for study be replaced by a ten-man panel to serve as a sub-committee to the Mayor's Anti-Discrimination Committee. Inasmuch as Rickey and MacPhail had not yet selected the two outstanding Negro leaders to complete their panel, they agreed to abandon the plan set up at the Cleveland meeting and become part of the Mayor's group.

With unexpected social-minded forces rising in several quarters, Rickey decided to accelerate a few of his own activities. Though he had a considerable number of reports on Negro prospects, he was concerned with the second and third conditions of his six-point program—those having to do with the right man on the field and the right man off the field.

Several sources, both by word of mouth and letter, pointed to a shortstop on the Kansas City Monarchs by the name of Robinson. A Sisler report declared unequivocally that he was a prospect and could reach the top, that he could run exceptionally fast, that he had a slightly better than average arm, though not a good one, and that he had tremendous possibilities as a hitter. Sisler also expressed the belief that Robinson's ultimate position would be on the side of the infield that demanded the shorter throw, the first base side.

Matthews' report stressed Robinson as a hitter with a high potentiality, due to the fact that he protected the strike zone better than any rookie that Matthews had ever seen; a great hitter for the three-and-two pitch. He concurred with Sisler in feeling that Robinson was very fast and he also agreed, much to Branch Rickey's dismay, that the boy might not have a strong arm.

The Rickey scouting system is based on three technical requirements, and a scout asks himself the following questions:

1. Can he run?
2. Can he throw?
3. Can he hit with power?

Since running is used both defensively and offensively, it is given double value in weighing a player's possibilities. The other two points have single values. None of the reports on other prospects seemed to match the estimates forwarded on Robinson. And there were many thorough inspections made and written.

Two of the strongest reports centered around the late Josh Gibson, the veteran catcher who had hit so many amazing home runs in Negro games played in the Washington Senators' ball park. But he was decidedly a veteran, and the reports on his activities off the field were not encouraging. Another was a giant of a youth named

"Piper" Davis, an infielder with the Birmingham Black Barons of the Negro American League. Though six feet four in height, and slender, he was exceptionally fast and could throw well, but his hitting ability did not have high promise. The veteran pitcher with the Monarchs, Satchel Paige, was never considered a candidate.

It might be noted that Larry Doby had a thorough inspection in subsequent seasons when the Newark Eagles played games at Ebbets Field. The scouting card declared that he was not a strong infielder and that his hitting needed plenty of minor league experience. Most certainly, the scouts agreed, he was not worth the $25,000 which Mrs. Effie Manley, owner and operator of the Eagles, asked for his contract.

All in all, the Robinson report seemed to stand out, even though Scout Matthews had declared that he was "strictly the showboat type." This meant that the boy was given to exaggerated display of personality which was common among Negro players at the time. It drew laughter, attention and sometimes applause. Often it substituted for a player's failure to drive in a needed run, though not in the box score. It made the fans forget the failure or laugh at it.

And so a third scout, Clyde Sukeforth, was dispatched for a final look at Robinson, and with orders to "bring him in!" Sukeforth reached Chicago in late August of 1945. The Kansas City Monarchs were scheduled to play the Chicago Negro Americans at Comiskey Park on the South Side, but Sukeforth reluctantly sent the following wire to his boss:

Branch Rickey Chicago, Ill.
Brooklyn Dodgers Aug. 24, 1945
215 Montague Street
Brooklyn

Player fell on shoulder last Tuesday. Will be out of game a few more days. I plan to see Columbus-Toledo series Sunday, Monday. Will have player meet me in Toledo Monday night and accompany me to New York if satisfactory to you.

Clyde Sukeforth.

Sukeforth, a tight-lipped New Englander, had been instructed to make the trip without attracting attention, if possible. He was still operating in the outward belief, if not the inner conviction, that perhaps Rickey was going through with his plans to operate the Brooklyn Brown Dodgers, a colored team, in Ebbets Field, with a franchise in the newly formed United States League.

Robinson's expressed reaction to the first approach by Clyde Sukeforth was one of acute distrust. In fact he almost laughed in the scout's sober face. It seems that many impractical jokers had made a point of representing themselves as big baseball scouts and it was a common jibe among the players on practically all colored teams. Robinson had been victimized on the college campus by a man who used the name of a millionaire as his own. Later investigation disclosed that he was janitor of a building.

It was always an embittering experience to Negro baseball players, for the spectre of never being able to play in organized baseball was a constant reminder of occupational futility. The appearance of a pseudo big league scout was salt in an open wound.

Besides, several Negro players had made unrewarding trips to big league training camps for what they believed were bona fide tryouts. Branch Rickey had entertained a pair of them at the Dodgers' training camp at Bear Mountain, N. Y., during March of that year. Three Negro players had managed tryouts with the Boston Red Sox in the Spring of 1945, but this effort was tied as a rider to a Sunday baseball bill before the Massachusetts legislature. A legislator swapped his Sunday baseball vote in Boston for a condition relating to compulsory tryouts for Negroes. An enterprising colored newspaperman, Wendell Smith, heard about it and wrote immediately for a trial with the Red Sox in behalf of three colored players.

On April 16, 1945 the Negroes worked out with the Sox at Fenway Park. Hughie Duffy, former Boston outfielder and holder of the all-time high batting mark (.438), supervised the trial and pronounced it "all right." Nothing further was heard from the triumph. The three players were Marvin Williams, 20 years old, a second baseman, of Philadelphia; Sam Jethroe, 24, of Erie, Pennsylvania; and Jackie Robinson, 26, of Pasadena, California.

It is of further note that Robinson's contract eventually was virtually beyond price, while the contract of Jethroe was purchased from the Brooklyn Dodger organization in September, 1949, for a sum in excess of

$150,000. Of the three, only Williams failed to reach the major leagues. Yet, each could have been signed to a contract for a song, regardless of who did the signing.

Little wonder, then, that Jackie Robinson was skeptical when Sukeforth first approached him in Chicago. Nor was he alone in his skepticism, for Sukeforth found that he wasn't playing.

"Well, can't you get into the workout?" the scout asked, "and make a couple of throws."

"I can't throw overhand," Robinson confessed.

"I just want to see your motion," Sukeforth persisted. "Don't make a regular throw. Just field a fungo grounder and make an underhand toss to first. That's all."

Robinson obliged in the workout and Sukeforth studied the movements, which weren't too good, but they were enough to indicate that the shortstop could handle a fast get-away from the "hole," which is that deepest part of the shortstop area toward third base.

There followed an effort on the part of Sukeforth to break down the player's skepticism, for Robinson was anxious to get down to the Grand Hotel on the South Side for his dinner. The inherent fear and apprehension, built by many decades and generations of distrust, was hard to tear away. Sukeforth couldn't tell any more than he knew—which was that Branch Rickey had ordered him to bring one Jackie Robinson into Brooklyn to talk about a contract.

Robinson finally melted, and arranged to meet Sukeforth in Toledo. From there the two proceeded to New

York, occupying the same drawing room on the train, and talking very little. They aroused no commotion and it was one of the most secret visits on record. Robinson was able to leave the Monarchs for a few days, due to his injured shoulder, and he had just about given up the idea of continuing Negro baseball.

With the noise of the train, the bewilderment produced by the cryptic aspect of the visit, the confusion of the subways, traffic and crowds, Robinson's head was swimming as he reached the Brooklyn Dodgers' offices at 215 Montague Street, opposite the old Borough Hall. Accompanied by Clyde Sukeforth, he appeared in Branch Rickey's private office on the morning of August 28, 1945. Rickey rose from his chair behind the mahogany desk as they entered. He came out from behind the desk, held out his hand and said:

"Hello, Jackie!"

He was a splendid looking athletic figure in Rickey's eyes, just a fraction of an inch short of six feet, 190 pounds of well-proportioned muscle. He was indeed a Negro. There was no doubt about it.

Rickey's agile mind traveled quickly back over 40 years to the Oliver Hotel at South Bend, Indiana, which had denied him the right as team coach to bring his big Negro football star at Ohio Wesleyan University, Charlie Thomas, into the hotel as a bona fide guest. It had been an humiliating experience, for Rickey as well as for Thomas and the rest of the team.

Rickey had been obliged to spirit Thomas into his own room, and the hotel unbent to the extent of installing a small cot in the room "if it was kept quiet." There Rickey had watched the colored athlete break down under the shame and embarrassment, weep with humiliation and curse the day he was born black.

"Damned skin . . . damned skin!" he muttered, rubbing his big hands hysterically in a futile effort to remove the layer that caused all the trouble. "If I could only rub it off . . ."

Here before Rickey was a greater athlete even than Charlie Thomas, who was now practising dentistry in New Mexico. But would this fellow be as fine and as great a man as Charlie Thomas?

Who was this boy? Oh, Rickey knew his name and his deeds and that he came from California somewhere . . . college . . . soldier. What was underneath, deep down? Who were his forebears?

That's the trouble with the Negro, you can't probe too far into his heritage. It's mixed . . . lost . . . clouded. And yet, you can't say that any one is or isn't what you want or need. If a boy hasn't had the opportunity, Rickey reasoned during this long silence, how can you say he will not live up to your expectations—up to your hopes? If he hasn't been tried, how can you say he'll be found wanting?

The scouting cards told his height, age and weight, how he went after ground balls to his right, to his left, back for pop flies, how he hit a curve ball, weight on what foot when he was batting, and whether the big end of the bat was still or moved as he waited for a pitch, his stance, his grip, his break and lead from the base when a runner, his school and college background, his aptitude, and many more things that the public least suspects.

And still it wasn't enough. Not for this situation. The first Negro in organized baseball had to be the "right man on the field and the right man off the field." And there was no way to tell by looking at him. Where on earth did his people come from? How strong was his character? Would he be able to take it?

Who *was* this Jackie Robinson that stood before Branch Rickey on the morning of August 28, 1945?

CHAPTER 3

UNDER any conditions, it is a tiring trip from Cairo, Georgia, to Pasadena, California. It is correspondingly harder to transport five little children and a few meagre belongings with practically no money. And no husband now. But Mallie McGriff Robinson managed such a journey early in 1920, driven by a determination to shake off the shackles of share cropping, and by a boundless desire to see her little children live and, perhaps, prosper. Daughter of a freed slave . . . now abandoned by the father of these little children . . .

Of course, it was Jim Crow travel all the way across Georgia . . . dusty and cindery day coaches . . . through Alabama . . . pick-up meals . . . a bit of Mississippi and all of Louisiana . . . diapers and restless children . . . fitful sleeping through interminable Texas . . . then parched New Mexico . . . Arizona . . . green and hopeful Los Angeles, and finally up into hillside Pasadena where Mallie's half-brother, Burton Thomas, had arranged for a place to stay.

Uncle Burton didn't have much either, but he could spare more. He led the six migrant Robinsons to a two-story house in the south end of Pasadena where the children crowded into cramped quarters not much better than the place they had left in Georgia. Yet, it meant everything to Mallie Robinson and her five fatherless children. It meant a kind of lung-filling freedom that you couldn't feel in Georgia. It was a quiet and comforting type of place, and she had made the move before the children were old enough to recognize the difference. Edgar was ten. Frank was nine. Matthew, called Mack, was five. Willa Mae was not quite three and little Jackie Roosevelt, born on January 31, 1919 and named for the late President Theodore, was fourteen months.

Though Mallie Robinson brought almost no worldly goods to California, she carried an indestructible faith in Divine guidance. With it she was able to defy misfortune upon rising at dawn. She used it as a bulwark in her endless day labor as a domestic, as a laundress, as a chorewoman. And it was a pillow for her weary head each night. It is doubtful that you could find a more unshakable faith in God and His intervention than has been lived and preached by the life and deeds of Mallie Robinson. Whenever one of the children raised the question about belief in prayer, she replied simply but firmly, "Prayer *is* belief."

No sooner had she gained a protective roof for her brood than she began work to get them more space and play room. All of her inconsistent earnings at first went for food and clothes. The older children had to be sent to school. And, as luck would have it, the California sun and fresh air seemed to increase the children's appetites. "They must have hollow legs," she sighed.

But within eighteen months, Uncle Burton had found another place. It was larger and the kids wouldn't have to sleep three or four in a bed. And so they moved to a somewhat nicer home on Glorietta Street where they had a whole floor of rooms for themselves.

And once again Mallie Robinson settled down to the task of getting her brood out of there, and into a "place of their own" where the children could grow and play and "not breathe each others' breath." It meant long hours and many jobs and the risk of leaving the children to fend for themselves much of the day.

But within two years she had achieved her goal. The six Robinsons moved proudly into a "home of their own" at 121 Pepper Street. They didn't own it at first, but it seemed as though they did. This was the place that Jackie Robinson was to call home for more than twenty years. Actually here was where his conscious world began. He was only four years old and he watched his three brothers and sister, all older than he, do the many things that he couldn't.

Edgar, tall and the oldest, could ride a bicycle like an expert. And tricks! No hands, and everything. He pedaled up and down the Pasadena hills with a speed that made little Jackie's eyes pop. But Edgar moved in a circle of older and active boys, and Jackie couldn't even tag along. So he latched on to brother Frank when Edgar was off riding his inseparable bike.

The days passed into weeks and months, and soon Mallie Robinson had to spruce up Jackie's clothes more to make him presentable for school. Presently another of her dreams had been realized. All five children were attending classes at the Cleveland Elementary School.

On a par with his love for the bike was Edgar's interest in and knowledge of the Bible. He had felt his mother's influence and had become a serious student of the Book. He could re-tell Biblical tales in his own inimitable language, and he did so when some kind of story was necessary to mesmerize one of the younger children at bedtime. Thus, Edgar took the place of the modern comic book, television screen, radio soap opera and other forms of juvenile preoccupation all in one.

Frank, next in line, wasn't too robust. In fact, he was inclined to be sickly at times. He couldn't go out and duplicate the strenuous stunts of the other kids in the neighborhood, and so he found an outlet through little Jackie. He spurred him to run, and jump and chase, and compete in games with the kids at every opportunity. In every physical encounter, which sometimes wound up with a threat of flying fists, Frank would be near Jackie to see that none landed on the little fellow, although Frank could scarcely batter back a swarm of flies, he was that thin and weak.

But soon Jackie's attention was turned to brother Mack, whose willowy endurance in running games provided the little fellow with more incentive than any of the older brothers could. He was long-legged, almost spindly, but with a rhythmic stride that ate up ground and made it look very easy. Mack was supposed to have some sort of cardiac defect. It was a murmur, but Mack heard differently.

"I thought they said 'rumor,'" he recalls with a laugh. "And I didn't believe in rumors. So I kept on running."

And the others kept on following. From Cleveland Elementary he went into Muir Technical High School in Pasadena, where Jackie recalls him as the greatest thing he ever saw before or since. He saw Mack make a shambles of all the sprint races in his final year.

"He was always my idol," Jackie says solemnly, "and still is. I don't think more than a couple of sprinters who ever lived could beat him at his best. And even then, I'd feel pretty sure Mack would come through. Six feet two inches and only a hundred and sixty pounds, and you could see every muscle working for him in a race."

Even Willa Mae not only liked athletics, but often expressed regret that she wasn't a boy. She was fast, but the dresses hampered her technique. Being only two years older than Jackie, Willa Mae was a sort of perpetual baby sitter while the older boys were at school or performing odd jobs and while Mallie Robinson was working early and late to keep the stream of food pouring on to the family table. And a semblance of shoes on the ten flying feet.

With five such appetites, there was seldom enough food for the crowded Robinson household. Eating between meals was an unfounded rumor. The supply was limited and spread thin. Hunger among the children was constant, and sometimes severe, because they were never still. Willa Mae and Jackie often went to the Cleveland Elementary hungry after breakfast. When they were lucky enough to take lunches, they would break down midway in the morning and consume them ahead of time, which would bring pangs of remorse and more hunger at noon recess.

This was during the period of 1930–31–32 when the depression had seized the nation's economy and money was scarce. Even while walking to and from school, Willa Mae and Jackie, young as they were, would speculate aloud on what their hard-working mother would be able to scrape up to feed her famished brood that night.

Willa Mae recalls particularly well two teachers in the elementary school, Miss Haney of the first grade, and Miss Gilbert of the kindergarten, who somehow sensed the hunger of the Robinson children. Frequently those two teachers would share their own lunches with the two kids. Sometimes it was only an apple, but sometimes a delicious sandwich.

"I could hear the echo as it hit my stomach," Jackie recalls.

Small as it was, the generosity provided an unforgettable highlight in the drab lives of a couple of children who had been thrust into abject poverty and constant hunger in a world of plenty. Such experiences often cloak children with a philosophy of bitterness; so colors their lives that they become anti-social. Most amazing is it that the Robinsons took it in stride. None of them is bitter. Probably Mallie Robinson would have none of it.

"The Lord will provide," she reminded them constantly. "Reverend Downs says He's taking care of a lot of us. So do the best with what you got."

Next to Mallie Robinson's, the words of Reverend Karl Downs carried most weight in the household. His influence was deep and exists to this day.

And yet the world was filled with wonders for their childish ears and eyes. Since there were few Negro families in the Pepper Street district at the time, Jackie didn't know the meaning of the word discrimination. Color of skin was of no moment to him. It had nothing to do with cleanliness. That was a matter of regular washing, a subject on which Mallie Robinson was constantly dwelling. Skin pigmentation had not become a factor in fun at school. Being 'it' in a game of tag depended upon leg speed or the lack of it. Jackie was seldom 'it' because few of the pupils in the lower grades could catch him. Sometimes he'd feel a little conspicuous not being tagged, and to remedy the condition he'd allow himself to become 'it.' But just long enough to make sure he wasn't missing anything. Then he would tag someone quickly and continue his successful evasion.

Unusual speed afoot and quick shifting strides won him a place on the soccer team which was formed when he was in the third grade. So speedy and skillful was this little team that they challenged and defeated teams made up of pupils from the higher grades. They even went out and defeated teams from other schools, and it was Jackie's accurate booting that decided the issue many times.

And yet, despite his rapid advancement in organized

games and competition, the amazing accomplishments of brother Mack gave him a sense of inferiority. The feeling didn't hamper his movements too much. But it made Mack more of a hero than ever. He was filled to overflowing with envy when Mack went on from Muir Technical High School to Pasadena Junior College to become one of the outstanding sprinters in Southern California.

Throughout his grammar school days in Pasadena, Jackie Robinson had three enemies, and they prey upon all underprivileged children. The first was the constant hunger, which seemed to get worse as he grew older. Sometimes he would walk stooped over to ease the physical discomfort. Did you ever eat discarded peanut shells? It helps. The lack of adequate shoes and heavier clothes against chill mornings of California winters was nothing compared to that longing for food. A kid can find a lot of deposit bottles in the course of a day. He can sell a lot of papers, if he hustles. He can pick up change for running errands, if he does it fast and cheaper. But it was harder still to get home with the pennies and nickels. A bakery shop . . . a piece of bologna . . . a fistful of candy . . . and he just didn't get home with the money.

The second enemy was school. He didn't dislike classes or his teachers. Or even his lessons. But there were so many new things to see that concentration was terribly hard. Luckily he had older brothers, and particularly an older sister who was a regular shrew on the subject of homework.

His third enemy was idleness—time to be filled by an

activity. He belonged to no clubs. He joined no playground group. Scott's Methodist Church to which Mallie Robinson sent all her children had no funds for vacation programming. Jackie, along with dozens of other colored boys and underprivileged white boys, simply had to organize their own fun, their own teams and cliques. They banded together for communal amusement, with occasional mischief.

One of Jackie's earliest experiences with unmitigated discrimination on account of color came in the handling of the Pasadena swimming pools. And with it came an unavoidable reaction of bitterness. The city contained several such watering places, and Negroes were allowed to use the pools one day each week. Once a spell of hot weather had descended upon the city, Jackie sweated it out, but literally, because the six-to-one odds didn't change. And he waited with other colored boys for the blessed seventh day to arrive. Sometimes the heat wave would break on the night of the sixth day, too!

Some of these pools had been built with federal funds, and eventually the question was raised as to whether municipal authorities had the right to bar anybody, regardless of color, race or otherwise, from using public pools on any occasion and for any reason. The sight of swimming pools packed with white bodies for six consecutive hot days, and packed with black bodies on the seventh, provided startling contrast. It distressed some people not connected with the municipal government. Presently the issue was brought out into the open. Then it was brought into court and the court ruled that Negroes could use the swimming pools at any time they were open to the public.

"If it had stopped there," Jackie says, "I honestly think the situation could have been worked out without embarrassment. Just knowing we could use the pools was satisfaction enough, and didn't mean we were all going to rush out and take advantage of a ticklish situation. But no, it couldn't stop there."

The municipal authorities, believing that it was a subversive movement on the part of colored people, or their "leaders," within the city employment personnel, purged the payrolls of Negroes.

And this hurt Jackie Robinson deeply, because his brother Mack was a Pasadena city employee who had begun his career with a broom and shovel on the city streets. But at the very time that Mack Robinson was shorn of his job, he was wearing the colors of the United States in the 1936 Olympic Games at Berlin. And he was wearing them with high honor, too, for his rhythmic speed had enabled him to finish a close second to Jesse Owens in the 200 meter dash, and to set a world's record for 200 meters a few weeks later in Paris when he ran that distance in 20.7 seconds for the first time. Mack Robinson returned to this country an athletic hero who had lost his job for being a Negro.

It was ironic to Jackie Robinson, then in his late teens, and thoroughly incomprehensible to his hero-worshipping mind. How could they do it to Mack? Wasn't Mack living defiance of Hitler's philosophy of Aryan supremacy right in Hitler's front yard? The sports writers cabled back the news that Owens, Williams, Woodruff, Johnson and other successful Negroes at the Olympics had given Hitler a real lesson in democracy at work. Jackie had read every line of it while hunting for Mack's name.

Nothing that happened to Jackie Robinson before or since could better emphasize the fact that he was underprivileged in more ways than one. He knew how hard brother Mack had worked to become a city employee and, at the same time, continue his athletic greatness—jumping better than 25 feet at Pasadena Junior College, winning AAU and National Collegiate sprint titles, and winning tryouts, sectional and final, for the Olympic team. Money and food were hard enough to get when you had a job.

Somehow the boys who lived on and adjacent to Pepper Street became more closely allied. Creating their own fun, inventing their own forms of competition, running in herds, collecting on corners as though drawn by a magnet, they soon became known as the Pepper Street Gang. This group contained the best runners, the best softball players, the best swimmers, jumpers—name your contest, and the Pepper Street Gang could beat you at it. As a gang, they were constantly hungry. They could get into an orchard and out of it faster than any watchman or guard, and satisfy the pangs of hunger en route. They would forage each other's houses, but never touched Jackie's, because they couldn't waste time on an empty icebox.

Satisfying hunger and filling the crannies of idleness

on long Summer days was a guarantee that the Pepper Street Gang would get into occasional difficulties. But they were not criminals, and none became a criminal. They might have ended up wrong, had it not been for the understanding and constant supervision of Captain Morgan of the Pasadena Police Department. His intervention and kindly, though firm, warnings saved them from getting into more than innocent trouble. The Captain was not only on the lookout for their foraging sprees and their stoning of street lights, but he often dug down into his own pocket and gave them a dollar so that they might "buy candy and keep out of orchards."

The life, deeds and reputation of the Pepper Street Gang are measured by its one official encounter with the law that happened a few years later. They were coming home from a triumph at softball beyond the city limits, and they were riding in a car of ancient vintage and dubious mechanical consistency. Jackie Robinson was the acknowledged owner, probably because no one else would have such ownership on his conscience, even though they did chip in to pay for the gasoline used on the trip, and the fifty cents for patching the front right tire on the homeward journey. Jackie had stopped the car to let a team member off at his house when another driver, a white man, turned the corner. He jammed on his brakes and the rear end of Jackie's car assisted him in coming to an abrupt halt.

Immediately the driver of the second car cut loose with a tirade of abuse, which the Pepper Street Gang would not tolerate from an outraged orchard owner. The colored boys talked back. Moreover, one of them hauled off and took a swing and effected physical contact. The driver said it was a punch. Jackie recalls it well and says that it was a slap. Regardless, it was gasoline on troubled waters, or something, because the driver challenged with his fists, and then saw that he was surrounded by about 100 people, mostly colored.

Immediately he changed his tack. He issued challenges to be accepted in other parts of the city. But the Pepper Street Gang declined with thanks, as they had softball games, swimming contests and other commitments. They started climbing back into the dilapidated jalopy.

Once again the air was split with a roar, this time from an approaching siren. A member of the Pasadena Police Force, mounted on a motorcycle, pulled into the crowd and threaded his puffing machine through to the Pepper Street Gang. He began to make arrests right and left.

The hubbub heightened and the crowd increased. As fast as the arm of the law collared a colored culprit, he would yank loose and disappear into the milling throng. With his assertion of the law failing repeatedly, the officer's temper mounted proportionately as he wormed through to the side of the jalopy. Before Jackie could even speak to the policeman, he felt the barrel of a gun in his stomach, and the cop was yelling epithets and warnings into his startled face.

Within a few minutes Jackie Robinson was in the Pasadena Police Station, charged with blocking the street, suspicion of robbery and resisting an officer!

Friends who had seen the collision tried to intervene without success. When Woodrow Cunningham, a close personal friend of Jackie's, persisted, he also was threatened with arrest and silenced completely.

Thrown into jail, Jackie was denied even the chance to telephone a friend who would either vouch for him, or obtain bail or a writ of some kind. He was tossed into a cell and held for the night.

Unable to telephone someone until the morning, Jackie communicated with John Thurman, baseball and football coach at Pasadena Junior College, who reached the jail on the double. Jackie was taken to court and asked to plead. He pleaded not guilty. It was suggested that he might plead guilty and obtain a suspended sentence, but Jackie was wary. After the night in jail on trumped-up charges, he doubted that any sentence would be suspended. He wasn't guilty and he wanted nothing else on his record. The law decided that he could go free on bail of $25—for blocking the street, suspicion of robbery and resisting an officer!

From still another source came an offer of advice. This time it was the University of California at Los Angeles, or well-meaning individuals at the institution, which, having followed Jackie's athletic activities at Pasadena Junior College, was counting on his later attendance. They didn't want an "incident." It would be better, they said, if he didn't show up at the hearing and forfeited the small bail. They would "get to" the papers and have the case dismissed.

Jackie took the advice and it was a mistake. He not

only forfeited his $25 bail, but was fined an additional $25 for contempt. The newspapers not only got hold of it, but plastered the sports pages with it. It was on his record long before he even entered UCLA, and this event is always singled out to prove that Robinson "always had a bad reputation around Los Angeles."

CHAPTER 4

GRADUATING from Muir Technical High School in June, 1937, Jackie entered Pasadena Junior College in the Fall at the age of eighteen. Three coaches were rubbing their hands in glee—John Thurman, Karl Metton and Tom Mallory. And little wonder, because Jackie had already displayed potential greatness in every athletic activity he tackled. He was five feet ten inches tall now and weighed 175 pounds, and was still growing, perfectly proportioned, well-muscled and with good bulk. He began playing football, reported for basketball late, and then competed in track and field and played baseball at the same time!

At Pasadena Junior College they remember him for many outstanding deeds, but none left a deeper impression than the night he set a point-scoring record of 28 for a single game of basketball.

"It wasn't just the record number of points," a recollector recalled in describing the game. "It was the boy's sense of fair play.

"Coach Karl Metton had a good team. It may have been a great team. I do know that Robinson was great and he may have made the difference. He did this one time when he rolled up the twenty-eight points. That made him leader of the scorers in the Pacific Coast Junior College division. But one of his team mates, Bill Busick, was still in the running for the individual high-scoring honors. Busick later starred for the Navy teams at Annapolis.

"Well, the score was one-sided, so Coach Metton decided to give his first team a rest. He pulled out four players, including Busick, and left Robinson in there. Jackie could have run up at least forty points and put the individual mark up where no one could ever touch it again. But he took a time out and came over to protest.

"He told Karl Metton that he didn't see why he should be left in to score while Busick, who had a chance for individual honors, sat on the sidelines, unable to have the same opportunities. Metton said okay, and benched Jackie too. The kid wanted a fair race of it, or none at all."

One of Jackie's most memorable days came when he was serving the two masters, track and field, and baseball. Pasadena Junior College was after a meet-title in Pomona, while the baseball team was to engage in a struggle at Glendale, forty miles away. The five points from a first place in the broad jump were sorely needed. But so was Jackie's second-basing skill, and his batting power.

The solution lay in a car and the driving skill of Jack

Gordon, Robinson's closest buddy at Pasadena Junior. Serving as chauffeur for the day, Gordon sat patiently as Jackie tuned up his legs and then raced down the runway for his first leap. It was good for 23 feet 6 inches, and sufficient to win many a senior college event.

"That'll do it!" Gordon exclaimed impatiently. He gunned the motor. "Come on, jump in."

Jackie picked up his sweat-shirt and started. Then he stopped.

"I better not," he said with a shake of his head. "Somebody in this event might get lucky."

Whether it was luck or not, Jackie couldn't say, but two of his competitors bettered the leap on their first jumps. Thanking his stars, he went down the runway again for his second turn. Carefully he measured off the strides, so that his flying feet would hit the take-off board on the split-second desired. Then he charged down the cinder path, sailed into the air and cleared 24 feet 6 inches.

Gordon let out a whoop and raced the motor again.

"Let 'em rassle with that one, Jackie!" he exclaimed. "Jump in!"

But Jackie didn't jump in. He felt too good. He hadn't extended himself on the last leap. Suppose *he* got lucky!

And so, with Jack Gordon champing at the bit, moaning about the forty-mile drive, Robinson waited for his third and last try. No one was coming anywhere near his second leap. Came his third chance and he paced off the steps twice. He took a practice run to within a few feet of the take-off, shifted the sweat shirt marker an inch forward, and then walked back to the starting point. He measured the runway with a final glance, took a deep breath and thundered down the path.

As his right foot struck the harder take-off board, he pushed his 175 pounds high into the air, kicked his churning legs for the extra impetus, and threw himself forward as his feet struck the soft, smooth dirt of the landing pit.

He had cleared 25 feet 6⅓ inches for a new junior college record and, in that year, among the ten best jumps of all time. It is still a performance rarely approached in college competition. Only—

It erased Mack's junior college mark of 25 feet from the book!

"Imagine that," Jackie muttered. "I have to go and break Mack's mark. Things aren't tough enough for Mack. I make 'em worse—"

"Stop beefing!" Gordon ordered and sped along the highway toward Glendale. "Get into that woolen baseball suit or you'll catch cold. Serves you right for breaking Mack's mark. The ball game'll probably be over before we get there."

Still a little sorry over the curious quirk in events, Jackie took off his damp track suit and pulled on the baseball flannels as the car went at full speed.

The game wasn't over when they reached Glendale. They arrived in the fourth inning, and Jackie was injected into the lineup immediately. It would be pleasant to relate that he won the game in the ninth with a homer, but it wouldn't be the truth. Pasadena was leading 4–2 when Jackie arrived, and his two hits in five innings only helped make the game a rout for his team.

The broad-jumping performance gave Pasadena second place for the team title and earned Jackie a trip to Lincoln, Nebraska, for competition in the National junior championships of the Amateur Athletic Union. There he outjumped the best of the nation's juniors with a leap of *only* 24 feet 2⅝ inches. This was a good jump, but it only emphasized the greatness of the Pomona leap.

A few weeks later, on July Fourth, brother Mack brought another gold medal into the Robinson household. Wearing the colors of Oregon University, Mack competed in the National senior championships of the Amateur Athletic Union, at Buffalo, N. Y., and lined up with the world's best sprinters for the 200-meter race. He tow-roped the field, breasting the tape in 21.3 seconds, ahead of Perrin Walker of the New York A.C., Ray Jeffry, a former national champion, and Norwood "Barney" Ewell in that order.

Honor . . . glory . . . medals . . .

And Mallie McGriff Robinson continued to work. Edgar had a family, but he was helping with the purchase of the Pepper Street house, and already eyeing the bungalow next to it. Willa Mae was married, too. And then Mallie Robinson thanked her stars for the preoccupation of daily toil, for Frank's life was snuffed out on the concrete highway. His love for a motorcycle had brought about his untimely death. There was nothing to do but go on, working for the others and the grandchildren, who were beginning to appear.

Jackie Robinson graduated from Pasadena Junior College in June of 1939. He entered the University of California at Los Angeles the following September, needing only two years of college for completion and a degree. Again the coaches were rubbing their hands in high glee—Babe Horrell, football, who had been All-America for California in 1924; Wilbur Johns, basketball; Harry Trotter, track and field; and Jim Schaeffer, coach of baseball. The UCLA Director of Athletics, Bill Spaulding, was wondering whether the college had done the right thing in admitting the boy.

"He was so good at everything," Spaulding recalls dryly, "I was afraid our four coaches would start fighting among themselves."

The fear was entirely justified, though not because the coaches were partial to their respective teams and the quality thereof. Jackie Robinson's natural aptitude asserted itself from the time he first covered his supple physique with UCLA's Blue and Gold for practice on the football field.

Babe Horrell knew, of course, that the Pasadena Junior had speed to spare on the gridiron. Jackie had made a few "all" teams, and the Sunday sports sections had frequently devoted paragraphs to his dexterity. But now Robinson was beginning major college competition. The stakes were larger, and so were the opposing players. The bruises would be bigger and the aches would last longer.

Besides, there was another colored boy on the squad—Kenneth Washington, a tall, well-muscled 200-plus-pounder, with power and determination, and a high knee-action not to be found anywhere on the Pacific Coast football fields. It didn't seem possible that anybody could compete with Kenny Washington when it came to plowing through a line or shaking off would-be tacklers in an open field.

And it wasn't possible. But Horrell made certain that Washington and Robinson never actually competed. Rather, he made them complement each other on the field by assigning them different chores. Washington was a powerhouse, a matchless, driving runner, a vicious charger who made tackling a hazardous undertaking. The high knee-action made you think twice before flying at him. By that time Washington was past you. His power through a line was devastating.

In marked contrast, Jackie Robinson could weave a dazzling pattern with his large but agile feet and the marvelous dexterity of his tireless legs. He would look one way and go another. He could twist his body into a forward-moving position, and move sideways. He had no mercy on his knees or ankles. He forgot them, so great was his concentration on the competitive task at hand.

And he ran so fast that you simply couldn't check for sure on whether or not the ball was actually tucked in behind his folded arms. You simply had to hit the trail, try to catch up with him and hunt for the ball. And more than half the time he didn't even have it.

His straightaway speed was great, though not the greatest. He was, at best, perhaps a 9.8 seconds man in the 100-yard dash. That is unusually fast for a football player, and, had he trained for sprinting alone, he might have been clocked in 9.7 or 9.6. The value of his speed rested with his ability to zig when the other fellow was zagging, and still retain his high momentum. He could turn on a dime and pick up the coin while pirouetting.

Coach Horrell employed the highly elastic T-formation system of attack. Significantly enough, one of the T-formation originators, Clark Shaughnessy, was head coach at despised Leland Stanford University, always a championship threat. But more important than any football system are the boys who play it, and it looked as though Horrell had come up with the right boys.

The T-formation style of attack is built upon speed and deception. The quarterback crouches directly behind the center of a balanced line. The halfbacks stand about four and a half yards behind the tackles and the fullback about the same distance behind the center. One of these three backs in the rear can move before the ball is passed from center to quarterback, and therein lies the elasticity of the T-formation, because this "man in motion" can run laterally to either side. The defense must spread to cover him, since he is eligible to receive a lateral pass or a forward pass.

Horrell set up Washington as his big powerhouse threat through the line, up the middle or off tackle or even end-around. He set up Jackie Robinson as his man in motion, and the Pasadena Flyer's ability was so diversified, that he was a threat behind the line as an occasional plunger or passer. He could kick field goals, too, and he might have served as water boy, but for the fact that the volunteers for that job were ample. Leo Cantor completed Horrell's power in the backfield.

Robinson's speed decided the first big game of the Bruins' season. With the University of Washington holding them even at 7–7, Jackie picked a punt out of the air and began an elusive dash from his own 30-yard line, zigging while the other fellow was zagging. Threading his path through the entire Huskie team, except one, he was caught with the goal stripe in sight, and dragged down on the Washington five-yard line. But that was the ball game. The Bruins carried it over, kicked for the point and won the game, 14 to 7.

Stanford had scouted the Washington-UCLA game well, noting the jack-rabbit quality of Robinson's field technique. Here was a new gridiron factor to be reckoned with, and the Indians were ready for him when the boys from Westwood appeared in Stanford's stadium at Palo Alto the following Saturday.

Early in the game he frightened a few years out of Stanford fans by taking the ball on his own 14-yard line, and sizzling down the field for a gain of 52 yards, only to be hauled to the grass by the Indian safety. Stanford stiffened and the Bruins lost the ball on downs at the 36-yard mark.

It was then that left-handed Frankie Albert started tossing hither and yon with the greatest of ease. He was playing the first of three great years that were to make him a football immortal. He could run, pass or kick with equal skill, and Jackie saw his first great exhibition of masterful deception.

Robinson played both offense and defense, and on the latter he had his special assignments, usually a particular take-out when Albert had the ball. It gnawed him deep to see this sleight-of-hand artist repeating the same tricks. It was particularly galling when Albert's passing resulted in one touchdown and then another.

Jackie was having a good day, but he couldn't seem to break completely loose and go all the way. UCLA seemed to be lucky to hold Albert in check while scoring a single touchdown. They were in the fourth quarter with the score 14 to 7. Albert's passes were protecting the lead—passes and his deception. Jackie noticed that Albert was following a pattern of procedure as the Indians marched slowly toward the Bruins' goal line and a third touchdown.

And so he gambled that Albert wasn't experienced enough to vary his pattern. Jackie ditched his defensive assignment on the next pass play. He leaped skyward in his own territory, speared the flying ball and started churning his itchy feet before he reached the ground again. He twisted loose from a would-be tackler, and dived for the clear, and cut back to run a diagonal for the Stanford goal.

They fooled him once more, because the diagonal is longer than the safety man's straightaway march. Once again they hauled him down on Stanford's eight-yard line, after a breath-taking run of 51 yards. But the Bruins were fired now, and Leo Cantor bulled over for the touchdown to make it 14–13.

Then, with the stands hushed, Jackie Robinson hauled his right foot back and booted the ball over the bar to tie the score!

Montana was victimized the next week, and a week after that Jackie Robinson went wild on the football field against the University of Oregon. He took a 25-yard pass from Kenny Washington and raced 23 yards for a touchdown. Later in the game he out-footed eleven of the Webfooters in a field-length dash that measured 82 yards after he had crossed the goal line. It was Jackie Robinson day, as UCLA rolled up her fourth victory, with only the Stanford tie to mar the perfect record.

Washington State was next. Robinson took another 25-yard pass from Kenny Washington, and raced over the Cougars' goal line for a touchdown. Later he sewed up the rout with a 35-yard run for still another touchdown. The final score was 24 to 7.

A victory over California in Berkeley made it six wins and a tie and every UCLA student was looking at the world through Rose Bowl colored glasses. The rest of the schedule wasn't too tough—Santa Clara, Oregon State and University of Southern California.

But a scrimmage just before the Santa Clara game laid Jackie Robinson low. His reckless abandon played havoc with his left ankle. A sprain halted his great speed and twisting deception.

Gone also was the Bruins' hopes for more victories. They weren't defeated. They tied all three remaining games, and fashioned UCLA's first undefeated season. But Southern California was voted into the Rose Bowl to play Duke.

Despite his crippled condition in those last three games, Jackie's first year of college football went into the records as one of the best ever seen in Pacific Coast gridiron history. He had scored four touchdowns and kicked two of four points after touchdown to account for 26 of his team's 127 points. He ranked tenth in total offense, which includes passing. But he was third in individual offense, for he gained a total of 519 yards rushing and had averaged 12.24 yards every time he got his hands on the ball.

He was second in total yardage for running back punts in the Far West with 281 yards, but his average of 20.07 yards per carry for 14 tries was a record for American college football.

The UCLA basketball coach, Wilbur Johns, was a man of infinite patience, and yet he was pacing the floor. He was ready to nibble his nails to the knuckles. He had started the basketball season, of course, while the football season was in progress. By the time he got his hands on Jackie Robinson, eight or ten games had been played.

And there was the strain of wondering when or if this athletic prize would be injured. Actually the left ankle was still a little tender.

"That's all right, Mr. Johns," Jackie reassured him. "I'll just pivot on my right foot."

But that was Jackie Robinson, take it from Wilbur Johns, now Director of Athletics at UCLA.

"If Jackie hadn't played football," Johns declared, "he might have been the greatest of all basketball players. His timing was perfect. His rhythm was unmatched. He had the valuable faculty of being able to relax at the proper time. He was always in perfect condition—never drank or smoked—and he always placed the welfare of his team above his chance for greater stardom."

CHAPTER 5

DESPITE his late start, and the tender ankle, Jackie Robinson sailed into the basketball season and, playing right forward, he competed in twelve games. Again he was an athletic marvel, and particularly so against the despised rivals, Stanford and the California Bears.

The Bears had their downstate brothers beaten, until a late game rush by UCLA brought the score to a tie. Then, with seconds to go, Jackie Robinson broke loose, pushed through the basket that made the score 35–33, and created the biggest upset of the Pacific Coast basketball season.

The high spot to Jackie that first year wasn't the victories and the high scoring. It came on Christmas Eve when the basketball team, dog tired from a hard but victorious trip through the East, reached Union Station in Los Angeles. The time was late and the wild crowd, milling through the station, yelled a raucous welcome.

Waving and yelling with them, though not so raucously, was Mallie McGriff Robinson, crying a little but happy that everything was all right. Jackie rushed over.

"What're you doing here, Mom?" he puzzled. "Trouble?"

She smiled. "With a trip like that, how could anything be wrong?" she countered. "I've got all the stories about you with me. You can read them on the way home."

She had followed every mile of the team's trip, clipped each box score and underlined the good things the Associated Press had written about her baby boy.

The season's high spot to Coach Wilbur Johns came in the Stanford game, played late in the season at Westwood.

"Jackie's chief rival for individual scoring honors was Ralph Vaughn, of Southern Cal," Johns relates. "They were running neck and neck and creating all kinds of excitement in Los Angeles—all over the Pacific Coast. Then came our game with Stanford, who had a high-scorer of their own, Don Williams. Vaughn and Southern Cal were playing California up at Berkeley.

"Jackie had another great night. He could rise to the occasion in uncanny fashion against our so-called traditional rivals, and he always played his head off against Stanford. This night his floor work was breath-taking. His speed, passing and deception sent our fans wild with joy. Stanford often put two men on him, and they held him to twenty-three points, but he played rings around Williams and outscored him. But that's not the unforgettable part.

"We all knew that Vaughn was going well up at Berkeley. The ticker in the press box said so. We knew that Jackie had to keep scoring to keep pace with Vaughn. He knew it, too.

"Yet, with the score close and time running out, he deliberately held on to the ball several times, instead of shooting. He'd set himself, draw the defense down near the Stanford goal, and then pivot and dribble down the court to freeze the ball, rather than risk chance of a Stanford score by shooting, and losing possession of the ball.

"Schools cannot teach that type of sportsmanship from a textbook," Johns says solemnly. "I wonder if we can teach it at all. I think so. At any rate, Jackie Robinson taught everybody the true meaning of team welfare before self that night. The whole gallery was yelling for him to shoot and pile up his record against Vaughn. But Jackie thought of the score and the team. Nothing else counted."

When the basketball season was over—and he had played only twelve games—Jackie was top point scorer of the Southern Division of the Pacific Coast Conference with a total of 148. He had rolled up an average of 12.44 points per game. He had beaten Vaughn!

Now two coaches were awaiting him with outstretched arms—Trotter of the track team, and Schaeffer, the baseball mentor.

Robinson had been in steady, competitive training for nearly seven months. He had kept up his studies, maintaining a C average, which is comfortably above passing at UCLA. But there was much more to his life than the athletics and the studies.

Much has been said and written about his "scholarship" at UCLA. It so happens that UCLA gives no athletic scholarships, for the simple reason that the university is a state-supported institution with an academic fee of only $35 a semester, a sum that almost anyone can afford. Nor does the school provide "clock-winding jobs" for the super stars. If they did, Jackie Robinson would have been entitled to employment of that type four times over.

Throughout his school life he was pressed for money. There was a training table, yes, at times, and expenses for necessities on out-of-town trips. But he was obliged to earn his own pocket money, funds for clothes, for fares on the hour-long bus ride from Pasadena to Westwood in the morning and from Westwood to Pasadena at night—yes, night, because practice was often late.

As always, his problem was chiefly financial, one that even his matchless legs couldn't hurdle. Mallie McGriff Robinson was still working, but Uncle Burton Thomas wasn't too well. He was getting old and Mallie was worried about him. Brother Mack had left the University of Oregon without graduating, and was working to help at home, because Edgar had a growing family and Willa Mae had a husband and a bright-eyed daughter.

Nobody could spare much, and so Jackie Robinson sought and obtained jobs as best he could from bureaus in the college, and tips from friends on the outside. But there wasn't much opportunity. He had sold hot dogs at the Rose Bowl games, which weren't many. He and Kenny Washington were lined up for bus boy jobs at the cafeteria of the Warner Studios in Burbank. It wasn't much, but it helped. And he was sure of eating regularly. That helped, too.

But he still hadn't figured out what it all led to. He didn't know why he was attending college, except to crystallize his knowledge of athletics and competition into the physical education course, in which he was majoring. The courses in political science and history were stimulating, but they didn't solve anything for him.

Yet, he reported for baseball and easily won a place on the varsity team as shortstop. He ran wild in the very first game for Coach Schaeffer. Playing against Los Angeles City College on March 10, 1940, Jackie did everything and did it well.

He walloped four hits in four trips to the plate. He stole five bases, including home twice. And yet the Bruins lost, 6 to 4, even though he fielded perfectly.

It was his one good day of the season. The team was mediocre and he couldn't seem to do it alone. He made only two more hits in the remaining ten games and finished the season with an average of .097 in batting. Ten fielding errors in 97 chances gave him the unimpressive average of .907, low even for a shortstop.

But he was virtually unbeatable as a broad-jumper, and his early Spring workouts were spurred by the thought that he could make the Olympic team and compete at Helsingfors. Two Olympic competitors in the same family! That would be something.

The punishment of football running exacted a heavy

toll from his rhythmic movements as a sprinter, and slowed him up just enough to make him beatable by UCLA's best sprinters in the short distances. He ranked about third or fourth among the speedsters at Westwood in an area that has always specialized in dash men. With ample protection in the sprints, Trotter urged Jackie to concentrate on the broad jump.

"He wasn't a good jumper," Trotter explains when questioned. "That may sound strange in view of his accomplishments, but I don't mean good in results. I mean in form and technique. He never had the time to specialize. But he could pace off a runway and hit that take-off with as much power as I've ever seen.

"Had he been able to train for broad-jumping only, and pace himself, there is no doubt in my mind that he would have broken all existing records eventually. That he was able to clear such distances after a heavy season of football and leg taxing basketball makes him all the more remarkable."

Specifically, Trotter refers to Jackie's first season triumphs for UCLA. He broad-jumped 24 feet 10¼ inches to win the Pacific Coast Conference title. Then he journeyed to the National Collegiate A.A. championships at Minneapolis, and cleared 25 feet again for a new honor, though a foot short of Jesse Owens' mark.

But the increasing fury of the European war precluded all chance of holding the Olympic Games anywhere, least of all in Finland, which had been invaded by Russia and later brought under Soviet influence by the peace treaty. Now the Soviets had recaptured the entire Balkan area in the name of Russia. There was talk of full collaboration with Great Britain, Lend Lease, military aid and a universal draft for American boys. With his final year of college coming up, graduation and a chance to earn long desired money, Jackie's startled eyes foresaw war and participation by able-bodied youngsters.

If Jackie was great on the football field in 1939, he was even greater in 1940. Unfortunately, the rest of the UCLA team was not. Coach Horrell couldn't muster the strength up front and the Bruins spent most of the afternoon trying to catch up.

Moreover, Clark Shaughnessy came up with a real powerhouse at Stanford with gigantic Norm Standlee, a greater Frankie Albert, Stan Graff and Hugh Gallarneau. The Coast team that beat this combination could beat anybody. But no team conquered that outfit, or even tied it. Averaging nearly 20 points a game, the Indians turned in a perfect season to tower above the nation's college teams.

UCLA began the 1940 season with a defeat at the hands of Southern Methodist. It was a real squeaker, decided by a field goal. The Bruins' only score came when fleet-footed Jackie caught a spiraling punt on his thirteen-yard line and staged a zig-zagging race through the entire Mustang team. He sped 87 yards for the TD!

Power-laden Stanford should have run away from the Bruins, but they eked out a one-touchdown victory, 20 to 14. Jackie was hot as a firecracker between the ten-yard lines, and the Indians spent most of the afternoon making sure that he didn't break completely loose. But

Horrell didn't have the scoring punch to capitalize on Jackie's amazing ball carrying. One good break and he would have scored the year's biggest football upset.

A week later Jackie played his greatest game of the dismal (for UCLA) season when he rolled up the Bruins' first and only victory singlehanded against Washington State.

He forward-passed for the first touchdown. Later he broke to his left on a handoff, crouching deceptively as he raced at full speed. Turning in sharply as the Cougar end spread to cover, he twisted from the secondary, outfooted the safety man to gain the clear. There he was uncatchable, and he covered a total of sixty yards in one of the most brilliant runs of the season.

But he wasn't through. Couldn't afford to be. The Cougars were able to score and the Bears needed more points. With the scoreboard showing UCLA with a one-point lead, 27–26, late in the final quarter, Jackie took a shovel-pass from quarterback, drove through off right tackle behind great interference, and then—

His churning legs did a pirouette, and he reversed the whole Cougar field; caught them slanting toward their left. Using everything he had, Jackie raced a diagonal toward the goal line. He had started from his own twenty-five-yard stripe. Panting and spent, he finished in the Cougars' end zone with a touchdown, and the game was on ice. UCLA's only victory of the year, against nine defeats.

But it wasn't Jackie's only big day. He came up with another in the traditional game with University of

Southern California. He helped stage a sustained drive from his own thirty-five-yard stripe, and wound up carrying the ball over for the score. Later he faked a run behind his line, drew the defense over and, when Ted Forbes was in the clear, heaved a perfect pass, which Forbes carried over for the TD. Inasmuch as the Trojans won 28 to 14, Jackie's contribution added up to a large percentage of the Bruins' offense.

At the end of the season, he had totaled five touchdowns and six conversions in ten tries for 36 points. And he had become something of a passer. He completed 41 passes of 98 tries, a percentage of .458, that were good for 435 yards. Supposedly a running specialist, he was third among the best forward passers of the Far West!

He ranked second for individual ground-gaining, as his passing yardage, added to his rushing gains, gave him a combined total of 875 yards gained for a team that won only a single game.

Again he was second in total yardage for running back punts, with 399 yards, but this distance was gained in only 19 carries, which gave him a new record of 21 yards average run-back. That mark was not surpassed in American college football until 1947!

Reporting six weeks late again for basketball, Jackie found the team calibre somewhat parallel to the football situation. It was an inferior team to the 1939–40 squad by a wide margin. But Wilbur Johns was happy, and so was the team, to see the same old Robinson.

They won only two of ten Pacific Coast Conference games and only six of the full, 20-game schedule. Yet,

Jackie's scintillating skill was at the same level. Operating again at right forward, he totaled 133 points for the twelve games he played, which was good enough to make him tops again in the Southern Division of the Conference. He also led in game-average with 11.08 points per contest.

He wound up the schedule in a blaze of personal glory, running rings around the University of Southern California team, and scoring a total of 20 points for the evening. Yet, the rest of the team could net only 17 points, and the Bruins lost, 52 to 37.

Although Jackie would have given an eye or a limb to see the teams, football and basketball, check in with championship honors, there was compensation. Well, maybe it didn't—couldn't—erase the pangs of defeat. But it sure helped Jackie forget what had happened on the gridiron, and the basketball court.

She had entered UCLA in September as a freshman. She was tall, slender and seemed to wear a perpetual smile. She also wore her hair sort of piled attractively in all kinds of rolls. It glistened in the sun as she crossed the hilly campus at Westwood, or as she climbed the steps in going from one class building to another.

"Rachel," she said the first time he asked about her name, because he hadn't quite caught it at the introduction. "But all my friends call me Rae."

"Well, soon as I'm considered a friend, I'll call you that, too," Jackie said. "That okay, Rae?"

She nodded and smiled. He was glad she wasn't the giggly kind.

Funny, but he had never gone off the deep end for

girls. Oh, he knew of their existence. More than that, he had gone out with them, even while he was at Washington Junior High School in Pasadena. But it was chiefly on account of his mother. Mallie McGriff Robinson didn't like his playing baseball on Sunday.

"The devil sends you out to Brookside Park to play," she had declared emphatically. "And the devil sends the people out there to watch you play."

"Did Reverend Downs say that?" Jackie puzzled. It didn't sound like the kindly preacher at Scott's Methodist Church. Rev. Karl Downs was for anything that would keep a boy out of mischief. "*Did* Reverend Downs say that, Mom?"

"No . . . he didn't," Mallie Robinson confessed. "I said it, but I'm saying it for him, because with all those people going out to see the ball games, a lot of his pews are empty."

That was when Jackie coaxed his mother into a trip or two on Sundays to see the Brookside Park games. Out there in the warm sun, running, hitting and with hundreds of eager, laughing people rooting, it didn't seem quite so much the "work of the devil."

But Mallie Robinson figured that it would be better to see her Jackie squiring a girl now and then, despite protests from the Pepper Street Gang. It was a natural thing, and the Gang wasn't.

That was his best explanation (or alibi) for taking up so seriously with Elizabeth Renfro, the prettiest girl in Washington Junior High. And things happened without him realizing it, such as saving his money all week for movies and popcorn and a soda on Saturday nights. And his mother suddenly coming up with the best shirt clean and the slacks pressed when he least expected them.

But the economics of taking a girl around were staggering, especially when there was no regular work. Funny, but the poorer he was, the more conscious pride he had about it. When some of the other fellows flashed bills against his rattling change, the pride turned to shame, and Jackie wished with all his might that he had gone out with the gang, instead of Elizabeth.

Ways to make money! Honestly, of course. Conjuring the methods is a full-time job in itself. Knowing where old metal was . . . a sharp eye for a deposit bottle . . . knowing where the deposit bottle would be accepted for cash . . . fighting off temptation to lift milk bottles for independent dairies that bought them and didn't ask questions . . . errands . . . deliveries . . .

Where to go for money . . . with the girl and the movies or the dance waiting. A couple of times Jackie barely got together enough change to risk taking Elizabeth out. Thought for sure he'd have to send word that he was sick and couldn't make it. He was practically sick, too, at the thought of not having the money. But he always managed, and she never seemed to notice how much or little he spent.

But this one at UCLA, this Rachel—Rae, now—whose last name was Isum, she was more than okay, and she had lightened the hours after the football defeats in the Fall and the basketball setbacks in the Winter. She did it by dismissing the game, not simply discounting the defeat. She was too smart for that.

"You can't replay a single minute and change anything," she would explain matter-of-factly. "Except your temper. That will change—get worse—every time you go over a play that went wrong on the football field or a ball that bounced the wrong way. If a ball didn't go through the basket, all your replaying won't make it go through."

"How do you know?" Jackie would parry.

"I asked your coaches," she would counter. "They agree with me."

And then they would laugh and Jackie would forget the football bruises and the twinge in his tenderized ankles. And they would laugh a lot and talk even more and he would stop worrying over what "might have been" in those two dismal final seasons for the football and basketball teams. She was always able to solve things.

She lived over toward the South part of Los Angeles, not far from the University of Southern California and the Exposition Grounds, yet she traveled all the way to Westwood to matriculate. Her big brother, Charles, or Chuck, as they called him, was already in the Air Corps and figured to be an officer soon.

And Mallie McGriff Robinson liked Rachel. Oh, it was more than just liking her. Mallie viewed her as something of a Rock of Ages, a rudder, an anchor, a ship with an even keel.

"Nautical but nice," Jackie added, as his mother paused in her symbolism. But Mallie kept right on with her praise and out-loud hope that Jackie would realize the value of such a girl.

Well, Jackie had long since come to realize what a girl like Rae could mean to a fellow whose spirits got down in the dumps so often. Walking or talking with her made everything else seem unimportant. It made you want to keep on walking and talking . . . forever.

That was the tough part of it. Between walks and talks you had to eat, and it was a man's place to buy the food. Money again . . .

Brother Mack had got married during Jackie's final year at UCLA. That meant a greater financial burden at Pepper Street. How long was a mother supposed to work, anyway? How long was a family supposed to support a near-200-pound hulk of humanity who jumped and ran and played; who studied just enough so that he would be eligible to run and jump and play? All his life he had been hungry and in need of money.

Now he was hungry for Rae and her companionship. He could see more of an answer to human existence than ever before. He could see why his mother had invited so many girls to the house on Pepper Street; why she laundered the best shirt so often, and kept the slacks pressed and came up with a little extra change now and then.

He brooded often over the possibility of having made a mistake in passing up the offer from the Stanford alumnus when he was at Pasadena Junior College.

"Pick out any Eastern college," the man said, tapping his chest. "Any college, so long as it's not on Stanford's football or basketball schedule, and you can have a liberal scholarship."

The guy never showed any Stanford credentials. Maybe he wasn't actually an alumnus, but he certainly talked like one, and he agreed to guarantee any scholarship Jackie or his advisors named.

He had recalled that offer so many times! Particularly when he was bussing dishes at the Warner Studio cafeteria, or doing odd jobs over the week-end for what seemed to be a pittance. All this might have been avoided. At the "Eastern college not on Stanford's schedule" he might have had it easy . . . or at least easier.

Yet, he couldn't see how accepting the offer would have altered anything except his own personal comfort. There wouldn't have been any Babe Horrell, either, to point him for stardom and place the big football responsibilities on his shoulders. There would have been no sage and kindly Wilbur Johns to understand things about him that other coaches might not have been willing to understand. And there wouldn't have been any Rae Isum—

That realization always made attendance at UCLA and the turndown of the scholarship to the Eastern college the wisest of choices. But it also threw him into a blue funk about the future. What about a job when he finished college—*if* he finished college? What was Mack doing, despite college training?

Odd jobs!

Well, the government had programs for youth. They

needed leaders in calesthenics, games, gymnastics and competitive sports. It was called the National Youth Administration. You could obtain work at the college, though it paid only a few dollars a month.

In the Civilian Conservation Corps, the government paid more. It was a living wage. It was enough to support yourself, and send a bit to your mother to make up for the loss of Mack's contribution.

"I've got to make the move," Jackie confided to the understanding Wilbur Johns. "I've got to make it *now*."

"Of course, it's always best to get your degree, Jackie, Johns said, "but a college degree is only a piece of paper, if it doesn't help you in your chosen field. You wouldn't be the first to leave before graduation, and I'm sure you won't be the last. Many of them return later and complete the requirements for a degree. I sincerely hope you will."

CHAPTER 6

JACKIE ROBINSON was greeted with an avalanche of protests when he announced his intention of leaving UCLA immediately after the 1941 basketball season and taking a salary job with the National Youth Administration. It was a deep disappointment to his mother, and to Mack, and to the Rev. Karl Downs. But Jackie was firm and listened to no pleading to change his mind.

It was a situation that confronts almost all outstanding athletes, because most outstanding athletes do not have a reliable means of livelihood. That is why they are outstanding. Work for pay is impossible. To reach the top in any form of modern athletic competition requires many hours for daily and diligent practice, precision perfection and the most rigid observation of training rules. More important is that the top-flight athlete must have food and shelter without loss of self-respect or amateur standing.

Jackie Robinson, as the foregoing resume of his sports activities indicates, was more than an outstanding athlete. He was by far the greatest athlete in the history of sports at UCLA. He was and is the only winner of letters in four sports that the college has produced.

It is possible that Jackie Robinson is the greatest all-around athlete that this country has ever seen. "No, no!" will come the cries in the name of Jim Thorpe, the Sac and Fox Indian star of the Carlisle School under Glenn S. "Pop" Warner. And such protests will be justified, for Thorpe's greatness has never been realized or properly appreciated.

But a careful study and detailed comparison would give an edge to Robinson on best performances. It might be said Thorpe lacked competition, and was only as good as he had to be.

Admittedly, Thorpe was the greater of the two on a football field in his fashion, and his fashion was the single-wing offense, backbone of the famed Warner system. In'jun Jim was a fairly fast and shifty runner, in the open field or through the line. He was outstanding in a day when a halfback had to do everything. Thus, Jim ran with the ball, kicked it and heaved it passing well.

Playing the more specialized T-formation, and not carrying the ball nearly as often, Robinson was outstanding in his fashion. Perhaps he might have scored 25 touchdowns, as Thorpe did in 1912, under Warner and the single-wing system.

Given an edge in football, Thorpe's superiority ceases, and Robinson stands in a class by himself.

Robinson's sprinting speed and tremendous broad-jumping skill would have made him unbeatable in the pentathlon, which consists of broad jump, javelin throw, discuss throw, 200-meter run and 1500-meter run. Robinson would have beaten Thorpe by nearly three full seconds in the sprint, and by two feet or more in the broad jump. The difference in these two finishes would provide Robinson with enough margin of points to finish second to Thorpe in the three other events and still win. And Jackie could toss a discus—has in practice—farther than Thorpe's best mark. Both weighed about the same, 195-odd pounds.

The gruelling decathlon competition might be closer. It takes two days to run off the ten events: 100 meters, 400 meters, 1500 meters, 110-meter hurdle, high jump, shot put, discus, pole vault, broad jump and javelin. Robinson's speed again would decide the 100 meters, 400 meters, hurdles and broad jump easily.

He could finish close enough to Thorpe in the other events to hold his own, and the final tabulation would find Robinson with the higher total of points. This comparison is imaginary, of course, and perhaps unfair. Moreover, it decides nothing, except that Jackie Robinson's lithe physique may be the best this country has produced.

Thorpe never played regulation basketball. Robinson most assuredly did, and emerged as one of the game's scoring giants. Not the best, however, as he insists when you volunteer comparisons.

"Don't mention me with Hank Luisetti," he scolds.

"There *was* a basketball player, and I couldn't even carry his shoes!"

But Thorpe played baseball, and played it well. You hear only that he "was a sucker for a curve ball." Well, so are many players who remain in the big leagues. Thorpe joined the New York Giants in 1913 and turned in seven years of major league baseball. He was in two World Series, with the Giants in 1913 and 1917. He later played for Cincinnati and the Boston Braves. Remarkable for an all around athlete.

Yet Robinson stands head and shoulders over Thorpe as a baseball player, a great fielder and a hitter good enough to win a minor league and a major league batting championship.

Thorpe never played competitive tennis. Jackie Robinson won the Negro championship of Southern California!

The point of all this is not so much to compare Robinson and Thorpe as it is to frame properly Jackie's status in the sports world. At the very peak of athletic achievement, he was surrounded by lack of opportunity to earn a living. He had found a lovely girl and he couldn't even earn money steadily enough to entertain her properly. There was no way for him to express himself, except through the coordination of his matchless muscles. How on earth was he to find a place in life, marry, support a family, buy a home?

Atascadero, California, is a town of fewer than 2500 people that lies near the ocean, about midway between

Los Angeles and San Francisco. But the population had been considerably increased by the installation of a large government work camp. When Jackie Robinson inquired as to the derivation of the town's name, he was told that *atascar* in Spanish means to stop a leak, or throw an obstacle in the way. Thus, an *atascadero* is one who does the obstructing.

"I hope it stops a leak in my sinking hopes," he chuckled.

The National Youth Administration part of the set-up was installed in an old school, and provided hundreds of underprivileged teen-aged kids with an opportunity to learn a trade or develop an interest, or at least forget the broken homes from which most of them came. As it contained boys of all colors and creeds, Jackie saw it as an ideal instrument for the correction of the very factors that had so deeply influenced his own life.

He saw young kids with the faces of old men. They were embittered, callous and indifferent. He wondered how many would have been in the camp with a different background of family, economics and education. He saw kids in a new light.

As assistant athletic director, his work at first consisted chiefly of playing shortstop on the baseball team. The government agency realized the morale value of the game, and picked the athletic directors with an eye to their competitive experience. Another assistant director was Lippman Duckat, a bright-eyed fellow with a shock of curly black hair, who played second base alongside of Jackie.

They formed a great double-play combination from the start, and the kinship developed quickly to the "Jackie" and "Lippy" stage. Then Lippy hurt his arm on a hurried throw and it went dead. Jackie lost his double-play partner, but found a friend.

Rather than remain inactive, Lippy discovered that he could operate a microphone with a glib tongue and a quick mind. In no time he was the camp sports announcer and master of ceremonies for all shindigs. He was preparing for a particularly big shindig not long afterward and dropped over to Jackie's room for a visit before the festivities. To his amazement, Lippy found his friend sprawled on the bed, reading.

"What's wrong?" the announcer demanded. "Aren't you coming to the dance? You sick?"

Jackie grinned. "Talk sense," he scoffed. "They wouldn't let me in. I'm colored, remember?"

"You're crazy!" Lippy exclaimed. "Not here. This is the government. A national project. And you're in California. Come on."

"Look, why hunt out trouble and scenes?" Jackie argued. "I'm comfortable here. I'm reading. After a while I'm going to write to Rae. Everything's fine."

"It's a big dance," Lippy declared, scowling. "It's entertainment for the whole camp. I never thought about your color. Why should they? And I'll tell you this!"

He crossed to the bed and hauled Robinson to an upright position.

"You get dressed for this entertainment," he ordered.

"I'm the MC and you're coming with me. If they don't let you in, they've got no master of ceremonies!"

With a shrug, Jackie put on his best clothes and accompanied the indignant Lippy to the Recreation Hall. To the announcer's astonishment, the doorkeeper apologized and asked Robinson please not to demand admission.

"He won't!" Lippy exclaimed. "And you can get yourself another 'white man' for the microphone."

Several months of directing recreational work at Atascadero not only grounded Jackie well in all phases of administration, but he was more determined than ever to make it his major work.

Unfortunately the camp was closed. Then came a chance to play in the Chicago *Tribune* All-Star football game in Chicago. This was an annual charity game that had become one of the year's biggest. The country's best college players were selected to form a squad capable of facing the National Football League champions.

In that year, 1941, the Chicago Bears were champs, and Jackie accepted the invitation to join the All-Star squad. Always a sellout, the game permitted generous expenditure for transportation, living quarters and incidental expenses. There followed three weeks of good living and relaxation at the All-Star training camp, mingling with the really greats of football and a chance to play before the biggest gathering of folks Jackie had ever seen outside of the Rose Bowl. Soldier Field was jam-packed with 98,203 football fans when Jackie trotted on to the turf that night in late August, 1941.

But he also had the unenviable experience of mingling with the very best of professional football in George Halas' matchless Bears. They were very rough, too, not in the least afraid of running into people. They ran into Jackie, also over him, never around him. He could run around them, but seldom got the chance.

Operating mainly with a backfield composed of Pugh and Thomason, of Texas A. & M., Jackie Robinson and the year's outstanding halfback, Tommy Harmon, of Michigan, the All Stars could do very little. The Bears racked up the collegians by a score of 37 to 13, and it was one of the biggest charity gates of all time.

But the game drew attention of the professionals to Jackie's aptitude and, more important, his availability. Within a few weeks he was a member of the Los Angeles Bulldogs, a professional team with a few games to be played in Hawaii. It was barnstorming, to be sure, but it was also money. Hundreds of dollars for what he had done for nothing in college.

And while he was at Hawaii, Jackie received an invitation by cable to play on the All-Star basketball team as soon as he had returned to the United States. It gave him a tremendous feeling of well-being, just knowing that his skill was of value, and that being wanted was enough to make a person feel worth while in the world.

Upon his return, Jackie reckoned, he would put his football earnings in the bank, play the All Star basketball game, and then turn professional in that sport. It wouldn't pay much, but it would be enough to pay his way at home and look people in the eye and even—

well, it might pay enough to finance marriage, or a start at it.

Why not? He wouldn't find anybody better than Rae Isum. Better? What an understatement! Why, nobody would come anywhere near her for looks, and hair, and teeth and smile and good companionship. It was enough to make a person want to earn all kinds of money to insure such a future.

The football games in Hawaii were without incident and injury and only moderately successful. People were war-minded. You couldn't help it with such news coming out of Europe—Germany marching far into Russia, conquering everything in sight, and the American economy being wrought slowly but surely into an arsenal for the British and French and now Russia.

It was all very puzzling to Jackie Robinson as the Los Angeles Bulldogs boarded the steamer at Pearl Harbor in early December to begin their journey across the Pacific Ocean to the United States. For his own part, Jackie couldn't get back quickly enough and start on the basketball business. They could have their wars. It hadn't touched America, and no country was foolish enough to—

Terrible storm on the way. Jackie could hear it as the steamer plowed eastward through the blue Pacific, the Islands a day behind. Thunder on the left . . . on the right, too. It was quite a storm, woke you out of a sound sleep. Made you look out of the porthole to see if the rain was in proportion to the terrific thunder.

Jackie drew his sleep-filled eyes from the porthole,

half-blinded by the shimmering sun on the dancing waves of the ocean. The caps sparkled as far as the eye could see. The gulls were winging at the side of the steamer, some of them gliding on motionless wings and yet keeping pace with the speeding craft.

And the thunder continued, louder, it seemed. Jackie looked at his watch. It was past seven-thirty. With a shrug, he returned to his bunk, yawned and turned over to dream of a pleasant future . . .

Money to marry. Money to help at home, now that all of Mallie McGriff Robinson's children were married and raising families of their own. Money to buy a home. Money just to jingle, perhaps, in your pocket as you walk along the street with a light heart and a lighter step. Money to insure your own family—sure, he'd have one—of a future in schools, good neighborhood, and college. A man has a right to dream like this, even with the thunder roaring a warning.

It had stopped now. Jackie was pleased. The storm had passed. He dozed off to crystallize the more important aspects of his schemes, only to be wakened by a pounding on the stateroom door.

Jackie wheeled out of the berth. Maybe the ship was sinking!

"You better get out!" a voice shouted. "We may be attacked any minute. Pearl Harbor's been bombed!"

"Pearl Harbor!" Jackie whispered. "That beautiful stretch of paradise . . . Paradise . . ."

The thunder was made in Japan, for it was the Day of Infamy, December 7, 1941!

CHAPTER 7

Five months passed before Jackie Robinson received his "greetings from the President of the United States," in May of 1942.

Finally drafted, he was dispatched to the cavalry division at Fort Riley, Kansas. He was one of about a dozen Negroes in the entire outfit, and half of them were assigned to mechanized units. The other half were ordered to report to the mounted units. Jackie was put in with the horse group, a decision which mystified him, since he knew absolutely nothing about horses.

Moreover, the horses knew nothing about Robinson and cared less. All the horses knew was that somebody was puncturing their hides with vaccination needles, and this Robinson character had hold of their ears. The job was to shake their heads and whirl him around until the grip on their ears was broken.

And Jackie's job was to hold the equine heads still while the vaccination job was completed. Finally he learned the trick of twisting their ears, and that kept them quiet. He succeeded in mastering the horses before they conquered him.

After three months of basic training, Jackie learned that the Army was on the prowl for Negro officers. He applied immediately to enter the Officers Candidate School, only to be told that the quota was full to the hilt, and that he would have to wait. Time passed slowly, except during the period of a visit by heavyweight boxing champion, Joe Louis. Jackie struck up a lasting friendship with him, and has never forgotten Joe's generosity.

"He was the quickest fellow I ever saw in reaching for a check," Jackie recalls, "and whenever I'd try to pick up one, he'd snatch it away and say with a scowl, 'Jackie, be yourself, man!'

"It wasn't just with me, I learned later," Jackie continued. "He did it with all of us at the Fort. He was a champion and insisted upon acting like one at all times."

Robinson was admitted to OCS and finally graduated. He received his commission in January, 1943, and there the matter stood.

Months passed as he and other graduates from officers' training waited for assignment. There was a rumor that colored officers were needed badly, and would be given a chance in the ranks, but it was no more than a rumor for a long time.

Eventually, however, Jackie was assigned to Camp Hood, Texas, and the 761st Tank Battalion, Company B. He was thoroughly acquainted with horses and their idiosyncrasies, and so they planted him among tanks, which had no ears to hold. Jackie was among eleven officer-graduates from Fort Riley, and each was assigned the responsibility of a mechanized platoon. Jackie didn't know how the others would handle the situation, but he assembled his men in a line-up and said with unabashed frankness:

"Men, I know absolutely nothing about tanks. Not a thing. So, I'm going to ask you to help me out in a most difficult situation."

The soldiers stared back with open mouths, as the officer confessed his ignorance, and also admitted dependence upon them. Jackie pointed to a sergeant who looked as though he had been slugged at the base of the brain, when the lieutenant said:

"The sergeant is in command of this group. That is all!"

Jackie doesn't know what might have happened, had he been a tank expert and taken over completely. Whatever the hypothetical result, it couldn't have surpassed the cause and effect of his bland confession of tank-ignorance and the assignment of authority to the sergeant.

Somehow it seemed to weld the platoon into a most efficient unit, working harmoniously as a team, and twice as fast. The sergeant was an effective coordinator from one end to the other. During maneuvers Jackie was always in communication with the sergeant, as his tank was equipped with two-way radio. And the sergeant would explain this move, that deploying action, which mechanism to throw forward and which to hold back.

To Jackie's complete astonishment, he was summoned to the office of the commanding officer, Colonel Bates, and his first fear was that word of assigning the authority might have leaked out. Maybe he was to swap his shoulder bars for the sergeant's stripes.

"Robinson," the Colonel barked, "I want to commend you and your outfit on your work down here. You have the best record of all the outfits at the camp and I have you up for special mention."

Jackie gulped. Beads of moisture gathered on his puckered brow. What would the Colonel say upon learning that it wasn't Robinson's doing but the sergeant's? On the other hand, why did the commanding officer *have* to know? As long as everything had gone so smoothly, and all was turning out well and special mention was being handed out, why not just let things alone? But before he could argue himself into silence, he was talking.

"Well, it wasn't exactly Robinson," Jackie confessed. "When I came down here, sir, I was a horse expert, and knew nothing at all about tanks. So I told the boys that and put the sergeant in charge—"

"I don't care how you accomplished it, Robinson," the Colonel interrupted. "More important is that you got the job done better than any other platoon could do it. It's all that counts. You've found a way to make your outfit tops and that's all I ask."

Jackie retired with a salute and a face-splitting grin. He passed on the news to the sergeant, along with his profound thanks, and the non-com was just as delighted. He passed it along to the tank-men.

Colonel Bates was so impressed that he invited Jackie soon afterward to accompany him to the European theater as a morale officer. It was high tribute, and one that he never forgot.

But all the while this was going on, Jackie was nursing a bad ankle, holdover from UCLA athletic competition. He had sustained a bone chip in his left ankle. Change of temperature created a tightness and often pain. Actually, he was on limited duty. Limited also was the government responsibility in the event that the ankle suffered further injury. In order to go overseas, Jackie would have been obliged to sign a waiver of claim against the government for hospital service, insurance and any other petition for benefit in behalf of the weak ankle. Inasmuch as his mother was beneficiary of his insurance, he withheld decision on the overseas invitation.

The ankle was under regular scrutiny and treatment, especially during periods of inflammation. Treatment required visits to the infirmary and sometimes he was held over and ordered to bed.

It was during one of these visits that he journeyed over to the officers' club for a visit and, finding the place deserted, started back to the hospital. On the way he encountered a wife of one of the Negro officers, and volunteered to see her home on the bus, not far from the hospital. They boarded the bus near the officers' quarters and took a seat about half-way back in the vehicle, which was characteristically lighted with a 10-watt bulb.

Jackie was engaged in making small talk, telling of his bum ankle and speculating on the prospects of getting out of the Camp to a scene of greater activity. The officer's wife agreed that a change of scene would be helpful to all the soldiers, particularly with decisions of war being made thousands of miles away—

"Hey, you! Move to the rear of the bus!"

Jackie looked around. Very few people were in the vehicle.

"Yes, you! Get back where you belong!"

It was the bus driver, and he was looking into the rear-vision mirror and directing his command to Jackie. With a sinking feeling, Jackie looked at his companion, who was a colored woman of light complexion that could be mistaken for a sun-tanned white woman.

Through the clouded thoughts, Jackie tried to coax some kind of solution. The bars of his commission gleamed on his shoulders, which were covered by the uniform of his country, which was engaged in a blood-stained world war for survival. And yet, here was a bus driver taking it upon himself to maintain strict geographic boundaries in his 24-seat world on the basis of skin pigmentation. Small matter, perhaps, but not to the driver, because failure to enforce the rules at all points would jeopardize his job. He was just as conscientious in obeying the rules of highway speed, stopping at rail-crossings and collecting fares.

Jackie Robinson thought back to the thousands of miles he had traveled by bus from Pasadena to Westwood and from Westwood to Pasadena, and with never any difficulty, except obtaining tomorrow's fare. He had never been obliged to ride in the rear because of his skin. To make room at the front, yes, because his was a long ride and the short-trippers could get on and off more easily.

The Articles of War said nothing about a white soldier or a black soldier. When you pledged to give your life, if necessary, to your country, you didn't say whether the life was white or black. And the country didn't seem to care. Had they cared, the country would have mentioned it somewhere—in a designation, or an officers' manual, or a general order. But nowhere in his military training had Jackie Robinson been told by the government to do anything because his skin was lighter or darker than the other fellow's. Of course, he had been turned away from the shindig at Atascadero, but that wasn't military. This was, and he decided not to move.

What Jackie failed to realize is that the bus was a piece of civic property which, come war or disaster, was under the jurisdiction of municipal decree, which, in turn, was made within the scope of a specific right of a state to segregate the races. The state had decreed that "colored people should sit in rear." He did not pause to realize that a preponderance of Negro citizenship in Southern communities was fenced off by such decrees in all walks of life, and all rides thereof. It was the law.

It was just as enforceable as restrictions pertaining to robbery, assault and battery or expectorating on the sidewalk when someone was watching. Rightness or wrongness or unfairness on the basis of custom elsewhere did not alter the statute.

Jackie Robinson did not know that these decrees were not the result of sectional hatred, but a means of racial survival in an area where the numerical odds have always been sufficiently high to create chaos in the event of mass action or mass revolt against subjugation. Two-thirds of the nation's Negro population is concentrated within ten of the Southern states. They constitute, one-half of Mississippi's entire population, and 40% of Alabama's, more than a third of Georgia's.

The learned Dr. Frank Tannenbaum, profound student of the Negro's puzzling place in the stratified society of a Democracy whose expressed foundation is the equality of all men, has declared:

"The South gives indication of being afraid of the Negro. I do not mean physical fear. It is not a matter of cowardice or bravery; it is something deeper and more fundamental. It is a fear of losing grip upon the world. It is an unconscious fear of changing status."[1]

Jackie Robinson did not know that peace and social tranquility prevail in the South when the decrees of segregation are enforced and obeyed, and that they produce hatred only when violated.

That decree and enforcement of segregation might produce turmoil and bloodshed when found oppressive,

[1] Quoted by Gunnar Myrdal, *An American Dilemma*, p. 563.

is not a factor, for only the Negro has ever found the decrees and enforcement oppressive. In the segregation states, the Negro exercises a prerogative of observing the decrees and living in peace, or violating them and drawing a penalty therefor.

Having left the segregation state of Georgia when hardly more than a year old, Jackie Robinson was ignorant of the social decorum expected of a Negro in the South. He was not completely ignorant, however, because he had encountered discriminatory practice in his youthhood. He knew of territorial restrictions, of different attitudes toward different races and creeds. But he recognized these discrepancies consciously, rather than unconsciously. To him obedience was a matter of will, rather than hereditary habit.

He had been taught the principles of national democracy, and that federal power superseded the rights of states. Now he was being apprehended while in the uniform of his country, an officer with stated responsibilities, and sworn to the principles of his government.

And so he chose by will and the holy badge of his uniform to disobey the provincial decree of the bus driver who, in turn, was sworn to uphold the local segregation laws or find another job. Understandably, an employee discharged for failing to enforce the segregation laws would be unwelcome in any Southern employment.

"I'll fix you when I come to a stop," the driver muttered. He slowed down the bus and hunted for a suitable stopping place.

Believe it or not, this took place on the military post, and they were still within the confines of the post when the driver spied three uniformed Military Police and requested Jackie's arrest. Since the lieutenant outranked the MP's, it was necessary for them to contact the provost marshal of the post, who was a captain. Jackie recalls that the provost marshal was only too glad to become involved in the situation. He arrested Jackie and listened to the bus driver's report. He did not question the "prisoner."

The charges filed against Lieut. Robinson were: Conduct unbecoming an officer. Disrespect to a ranking officer. The provost marshal demanded a court martial and Jackie was ordered to trial.

By ordinary standards, the arrest and court martial of Jackie Robinson at Camp Hood, Texas, was an outrage. By sectional standards it is most understandable. If there existed a statute in a Northern state wherein the use of a Southern dialect in public speech were a misdemeanor or worse, arrest and trial for violation would result in national ridicule. But the statute would be defended by the penalizing state. And only good luck would save the Southern dialectician from a prison sentence or stiff fine.

Robinson had violated the basic principle of segregation through the establishment of physical proximity. For only by maintenance of racial segregation can supremacy be identified. Therein lies the reason for ordering colored people to the rear of a Southern bus. Neither Robinson, nor any group in experiment or defiance, can break down the practice by riding in the middle of the bus or in the front, for the reason that riding in the middle or the front does not change the basic reason for the rule. The reason continues to exist, even if Negroes ride on the roof or sit on the driver's lap.

Arresting and court martialing a Negro officer for failing to obey a command based on local segregation laws would sound silly in any military report. It might even sound unconstitutional and be regarded as such. And so Lieut. Robinson wasn't so charged. He was accused of "conduct unbecoming an officer and showing disrespect for a ranking officer." To support these charges, the provost marshal declared that:

Lieut. Robinson had used profane language in the presence of a woman on the bus, not his companion, but a kitchen-worker from the military post who happened to be a passenger on the bus.

Lieut. Robinson had disobeyed his superior officer, though details were not stated, by disregarding an order.

Lieut. Robinson had been disrespectful to a superior officer by cupping his chin in his hands and leaning his elbows on the desk.

Understandably, there was no mention of his failure to take a seat in the rear of the bus when ordered to do so by the driver.

But Jackie was not without friends. The wife of the colored officer and the officer himself rushed to his side. They pleaded with him to contact the National Association for the Advancement of Colored People and all the newspapers. But Jackie stubbornly refused.

"Nuts!" he declared heatedly. "If this is what they

want to do with me, okay. I've gone through all this before. I can stand it again."

He refused to register complaint against anybody. But the colored officer and his wife acted on their own initiative. They wrote to one of the Pittsburgh papers, relating the outrage, and the newspaper wrote to the authorities at Camp Hood, demanding the facts.

In the days immediately preceding the court martial, the provost marshal decided to reconsider the charges. To Jackie's astonishment, and good luck, the indictment was altered completely. He was now hauled to the bar of military justice charged with "insubordination and wilful disobedience." The penalty in the event of guilt would be limited to a fine.

For his defense, Jackie was assigned a Southern lawyer with white skin, who did not remain on the case long. He came to Jackie and confided that he couldn't handle the situation without prejudice, and brought in another officer to plead the case. The new defender took the accusing captain by the scruff of the neck, figuratively, of course, and wiped up the court room with him. He broke contact between the provost marshal and the MP's and the bus driver and they never did get their stories or the charges to coincide.

Colonel Bates testified in Jackie's behalf, and so decidedly in his behalf, that the officer in charge of the court proceedings objected to his testimony. The Colonel was charged with being prejudiced in the "prisoner's" behalf. The Colonel not only admitted it, but declared that he was on the side of any fine soldier who had done the job that Lieut. Robinson had accomplished at Camp Hood, both in military tactics and morale. In fact, he declared, he still hoped to have Lieut. Robinson on his staff in the European theater of war!

And so Jackie was completely exonerated by the military court. But the ankle with the chipped bone continued to act up and Jackie had to do a stretch in the hospital. When he was discharged, his outfit had gone overseas, and he was subsequently transferred to Camp Breckenridge. He assisted with recreational programs until December, 1944, at which time he was given an honorable discharge due to the condition of his leg. He had been in uniform for thirty-one months, and away from California that long, except for a couple of brief furloughs.

At Pasedena he found a letter from Rev. Karl Downs, the old minister from Scott's Methodist Church.

"He's president of a college," Mallie Robinson declared, beaming. "He wants you to work with him."

At first Jackie thought this might be a plea for him to enter the ministry—an old dream of his mother's. But it wasn't. Dr. Downs was president of Sam Houston College, at Austin, Texas. There was much work to be done to help the colored boys in the college. Jackie could be athletic director and, at the same time—

"You can complete the requirements for your degree," Dr. Downs said. "You should finish what you start. If you are to work with young boys, you must be a model for them. You cannot be the fellow who 'almost finished college.' They might feel that almost finishing is enough, and it never is."

There wasn't a chance in the world for Jackie to refuse. The hopeful look in his mother's eyes, and the sincere appeal of Rev. Downs—well, the only thing to do was accept. He would have taken it anyway, because it was a chance to work with growing boys and help them over some of the rough spots that he couldn't avoid.

Sam Houston College boasted a small enrollment of Negro students, less than half of whom were males, and very few of whom were interested in basketball, the sport that Jackie decided to feature. When the tryouts and evaluation of ability were completed, the "squad" consisted of only seven players. But it was a start.

And within a few weeks after Jackie had worked with them, they were a team. He patterned his instructional methods after Wilbur Johns, stressing patience and understanding. The game was new to most of the boys, but they possessed aptitude and an eagerness to compete. That is half of a coach's problem anyway, and the basketball team prospered.

The remainder of the athletic program was quite limited, for so were the college's funds. Jackie's salary was low, as was his supply of equipment, but he stretched everything and enjoyed the satisfaction of launching a program for the old family friend and counsellor, Dr. Downs. Moreover, Jackie's basketball team had the satisfaction of beating Bishop College for the city title, 61 to 59!

But the post at Sam Houston College barely paid a living wage. The money simply wasn't there. How *do* the Negro colleges obtain money? Jackie pondered the question without finding an answer. If Negroes have a tough time obtaining money for food, clothes and shelter, they have an even tougher time contributing to college endowments. It was something to remember.

That was why he cast his eye about for a means of livelihood. There was Rae to consider. You can't marry a girl and expect her to starve with you. Or should you? No, you should go out and do your level best to get a threshold to carry her over. Pioneering is all right, for at least there is a type of shelter. Jackie didn't even have a covered wagon.

And so he wrote a letter to nearby Houston, Texas. Up at Camp Breckenridge he had met a fellow who once pitched for a colored baseball team called the Kansas City Monarchs. The team was always on the lookout for good ball players or, during war time, just ball players. The pitcher had suggested that Jackie contact the team, after he had shown a few abilities in the Kentucky camp. The Monarchs were training at Houston, and nothing could be lost through a letter.

Lost? It was terrific. The team's business manager, William Dismukes, replied with an offer of $300 a month for playing with the Monarchs. Jackie countered with a letter of thanks, adding that he couldn't think of joining for less than $400 a month. While he was wondering whether he had asked too much, and whether the opportunity would disappear entirely, a letter of acceptance arrived and he was a professional baseball player.

But the news made no one happy in Los Angeles, particularly Rae Isum, who had switched her college course to nursing when the war started. She was planning to complete her nursing course in U of C at Berkeley, thinking that Jackie would return there, after his discharge, and work. Joining a professional baseball team meant traveling all over and seldom, if ever, getting to the Pacific Coast. How were two people to know each other?

Jackie explained that he knew her, all right, as the very best there was, and worthy of the best he could get. He still wanted to send money home to his mother, because—

Well, Uncle Burton Thomas had suffered a setback —a shock, they called it. He couldn't get up and around. He should have been in a hospital, or a nursing home for better care.

"Nobody could give him better care than I can right here on Pepper Street!" Mallie McGriff Robinson declared with sufficient defiance to settle the matter. "He'll stay with me, and now *I* can take care of *him*."

Which she did, and still continued her outside work. It filled Jackie to overflowing with a desire to help. The woman evidently had no end of willingness to work and care for her loved ones. The spectre of bed-ridden Uncle Burton and his mother refusing to let them remove him from the house forced Jackie to take the most money he could get honestly. He assured Rae that it was only temporary. He would try to save. He would live frugally until . . . until . . .

He couldn't say, exactly. He didn't know what he was heading for. The war was almost over, according to reports. Germany had been conquered. The Japanese were on the run. There was no telling what the Summer would bring. Maybe Jackie could play baseball well enough to become a star in this Negro league. The ageless Satchel Paige had been a big money earner as a pitcher who practically dictated his own terms. That was because he could fill a ball park on a Saturday and Sunday, pitch both days and win both games. Of course, Jackie couldn't become such a drawing card ever, he explained to Rae. But he could be an important part of the show. He would play to win always, and play his best, colorful or not. And there would be $400 each month for the next five or six.

There was no contract. No security. But a man's word was good. Naturally, if Jackie didn't play up to expectations or even above them, they could cut him adrift. It was entirely up to his ability.

He lost no time getting to Houston and suiting up with the Kansas City Monarchs. He coaxed his ankle along slowly before testing it on the quick stops and starts and pivots required of a good shortstop. Except for a protesting twinge now and then, the ankle was sound, and he put more and more pressure on the underpinning.

Within a month of play he was scampering back and forth with all his old zest. Moreover, he was able to hit the pitching of this Negro American League, which played in Kansas City, Chicago, Birmingham, Memphis, St. Louis, Cincinnati and Cleveland chiefly, but anywhere a game might be booked.

He wasn't certain which game was for the "league records" and which was exhibition. They weren't sure of their itinerary more than a week in advance, and there were many cancellations and substitution games. Knowing the value of official records, Jackie would have liked to know which games were "for the record" and which were exhibitions. Unable to learn, he simply had to play every game for the book, night and day, week after week. He bore down every minute fearful that let-up might ruin his good batting average.

Good? It was the best. He batted around .350 from the start of the season, and kept the figure up there, despite a flock of night games in poorly lighted parks, all-night bus travel, Jim Crow hotels and diners, and the heaviest schedule of games he ever encountered. At one point he was ready to call it quits and so informed the management.

"I can't go on," he confessed. "It's worse than the tougest job I could get at home, and I'm not even home. I have no security, no contract, no insurance. I just can't go on."

Another $100 a month enabled him to continue, but the money didn't make him feel more secure. Nor did it improve the haphazard conditions of travel, living and playing. By mid-season they were talking about a Fall barnstorming trip. They'd get to play real big leaguers and bat against Bobby Feller, pitch to Joe Di Maggio . . .

Jackie chuckled. What a privilege! No, sir. Not for him. The war was just about over. Soldiers and sailors and Marines were coming out of uniform. The competition for jobs would be keen again. He decided he had better get back to the Pacific Coast and settle down at a trade, or some kind of coaching job. Anything but professional baseball like this. Anything could happen to you—

And it did. Trying for a hard-hit ground ball to his right, his toe cleat caught in the hard basepath and he catapulted forward, landing on his right shoulder. He felt an agonizing tear and lay on the ground wondering if the arm had been torn from its socket. No white-uniformed trainer rushed to the field. No doctor was waiting in the clubhouse. He looked up at two or three sympathetic faces, Monarchs of all they surveyed . . .

CHAPTER 8

JACKIE ROBINSON has never been able to describe his feelings as he stood before Branch Rickey in the quiet, air-conditioned office at 215 Montague Street, Brooklyn, on the morning of August 28, 1945. He can recollect only patches of reaction that appeared clear in the general blur of a most confusing situation.

He recalls the lighted goldfish tank and the piscatorial captives. He felt a little like the fish, as this bushy-browed, bespectacled man with the smoking cigar and knotty fingers seemed to x-ray him from head to toes. He found his gaze fixed upon the flame of a match which Rickey held aloft, preparatory to relighting the cigar.

He recalls that the furnishings were big and leathery. The desk was mammoth and littered with books and a box of matches and a humidor of cigars and covered elsewhere with sprawling papers. On the walls were pictures, one a pretty color-photo of a player throwing a ball. It looked like Leo Durocher. Jackie also recalls a lighted globe behind Rickey's head that seemed to place all his rugged features in a puzzling shadow.

The noise of the city . . . a cacophony of sounds . . . the riverboat whistles . . . the roar of the subway like that of an angry lion . . . the clang of Brooklyn streetcars (you could still hear them) . . . the whir of automobile engines . . . and human voices, too . . . His ears still rang . . .

"Do you have a girl, Jackie?"

Jackie blinked. He opened his mouth to answer, but the words wouldn't emerge. He struggled and then said, "I don't know."

"What do you mean, you don't know?" Rickey retorted.

"Well," the player stammered, "the way I've been traveling around the country, and not writing as I should—well, I don't know if I have a girl or not."

"Of course you have a girl," Rickey scoffed. "And you need one. Ought to marry her as quick as you can. But sit down." He pointed the lighted cigar toward an overstuffed leather chair at the right side of the big desk. "Make yourself comfortable. We have a lot of things to talk about, and we've got plenty of time to do it."

Jackie murmured his thanks and settled into the indicated chair. Somehow the cushiony leather didn't seem to relieve his discomfiture. He couldn't seem to chase the doubt from his whirling brain. He kept telling himself that this was all right. This was the real thing. Why be suspicious when there was no reason for suspicion . . . so far?

So far. That was it. The truth and reality of the situation, as it appeared, was only temporary. Soon the gimmick would appear. Soon the *real* reason would come to the surface, and he'd be double-crossed again, or exploited or maybe arrested and jailed.

It had always happened when you had something that another person wanted, or was afraid of. Why would this man choose to do something that the whole game of baseball shied from?

What was Rickey's percentage? How could he gain? Most assuredly, he wasn't doing anything just for little Jackie Robinson, or for hard-working Mallie McGriff Robinson. Why should a well-known and successful baseball man suddenly want to turn everything upside down and—? All the more reason why this had nothing to do with the regular Brooklyn Dodgers.

The conviction seemed to make Jackie feel better. He eased back into the leather chair and waited for the baseball man to speak.

"Are you under contract to the Kansas City Monarchs?" Rickey challenged.

"No, sir," Robinson replied quickly. "We don't have contracts."

"Do you have *any* agreement—written or verbal—about how long you will play for them?"

"No, sir, none at all. I just work from pay day to pay day."

Rickey nodded and his bushy brows meshed into a scowl. He toyed with the ever present cigar again, trying to find the right words for the beginning.

"Do you know why you were brought here?" he asked.

Robinson's head moved from side to side. "Not exactly," he murmured. "I heard something about a colored ball team at Ebbets Field. That it?"

"No . . . that isn't it." Rickey studied the dark face, the half-open mouth, the widened, worried eyes. Then he said, "You were brought here, Jackie, to play for the Brooklyn organization. Perhaps at Montreal to start with and—"

"Me? Play for Montreal?" the player gasped.

Rickey nodded. "If you can make it, yes. Later on—also if you can make it—you'll have a chance with the Brooklyn Dodgers."

Robinson could only nod at this point.

"I want to win pennants and we need ball players!" Rickey whacked the desk for emphasis. "The war set us back a little in manpower, so three years ago the Brooklyn Dodger management decided to scout untapped sources of supply—Mexico, Cuba, all the Latin-American countries—and our own country too. Is that right, Clyde?"

"From coast to coast!" Sukeforth declared with a sigh.

"Yes," Rickey continued, "for players who can help us win. Many of the boys we saw were good. Some had great promise—like you. Do *you* think you can do it? Make good in organized baseball?"

Robinson shifted to relieve the mounting tension.

"If . . . if I got the chance," he stammered.

"There's more here than just *playing*, Jackie," Rickey warned. "I wish it meant only hits, runs and errors—things you can see in a box score . . ."

He reflected at this point on the integrity of this statistical phenomenon of the sports page.

"You know, Jackie," he mused, "a baseball box score is really a democratic thing. It doesn't say how big you are, or how your father voted in the last election, or what church you attend. It just tells you what kind of a ball player you were that day!"

"Isn't that what counts?" the player ventured.

"It's all that ought to count!" Rickey stormed suddenly, rose from his chair and began to pace the carpeted floor of the big office. He hiked his wrinkled trousers and paced back to his desk. "Maybe some day it's all that will count. That's one of the reasons why you're here, Jackie. If you're a good enough ball player, we can make a start in the right direction. But it will take a lot of courage."

"Yeah," Robinson whispered. "It sure will . . ."

Sukeforth said, "It might take more courage for the Brooklyn management than for you, Jackie. Have you thought of that?"

Robinson shrugged. "I haven't thought of anything. It's all so sudden. It kinda hits me between the eyes."

"We're tackling something big here, Jackie," Rickey continued. "If we fail, no one will try it again for twenty years. But if we succeed—"

"Brooklyn'll win a pennant," Sukeforth finished.

Rickey nodded and smiled. "Oh, yes," he agreed, and

sobered quickly. "But we're dealing with rights, too. And courage." He turned to Sukeforth. "Do *you* think he's our boy, Clyde?"

Robinson's eyes seemed to pop as he searched their faces for the answer. He seemed to feel he was losing hope, and sponsorship; suddenly caged and alone.

"He can run. He can field. He can hit," the scout said.

"But can he take it?"

"That I don't know."

Robinson's eyes shifted from one to the other as the frank appraisal dissected his latent courage before him.

"What do you think, Jackie?" Rickey asked.

"I . . . I can try," the player whispered.

Rickey leaned close and spoke with a crescendo of feeling.

"You think you've got the guts to play the game no matter *what* happens?" Rickey demanded. "They'll shout insults at you. They'll come into you spikes first. They'll throw at your head!"

"Mr. Rickey," he said bitterly, "they've been throwing at my head for a long time."

Rickey's voice rose. "Suppose I'm a player . . . in the heat of an important ball game." He drew back and prepared to charge at the Negro. "Suppose I collide with you at second base. When I get up, I yell, 'you dirty, black son of a—' " He finished the excoriation and then said calmly, "What do you do?"

Robinson blinked. He licked his heavy lips and swallowed.

"Mr. Rickey," he puzzled. "Do you want a ball player who's afraid to fight back?"

"I want a ball player with guts enough *not* to fight back!" Rickey exclaimed almost savagely. He paced across the floor again and returned. "You've got to do this job with base hits and stolen bases and fielding ground balls, Jackie. *Nothing else!*"

He moved behind his big desk again and faced the cornered Robinson. He posed as a cynical clerk in a southern hotel who not only refused sanctuary, but handed an invective with it. What would Robinson do? He posed as a prejudicial sports writer, ordered to turn in a twisted story, full of bias and racial-baiting. How would Robinson answer the sports writer? He ordered the player from imaginary dining rooms. He jostled him in imaginary hotel lobbies, railroad stations. What would Robinson do?

"Now I'm playing against you in the World Series!" Rickey stormed and removed his jacket for greater freedom. Robinson's ebony hands were beginning to clench from the rising tension. "I'm a hot-headed player. I want to win that game, so I go into you spikes first. But you don't give ground. You stand there and you jab the ball into my ribs and the umpire yells, 'Out!' I flare—all I see is your face—that black face right on top of me—"

Rickey's bespectacled features were inches from Robinson's face at this point. He yelled into the motionless mask.

"So I haul off and punch you *right in the cheek!*"

An oversized white fist swung through the air and barely missed Robinson's sweating face. The dark eyes blinked, but the head didn't move.

"What do you do?" Rickey roared.

The heavy lips trembled for an instant and then opened.

"Mr. Rickey," he whispered. "I've got *two* cheeks . . . that it?"

Rickey nodded and blinked away the mist from his own eyes. He returned to his desk, picked another cigar from the humidor, tore off the end and tossed it to the floor. He studied the glistening face and watched the big, dark fist, still grinding into the left palm. This *had* to be the right boy, on the field and off. Who else?

There was much to talk about. They'd be busy for another hour, perhaps two more, discussing the finer points. But nothing that this colored boy could say would make more firm Rickey's deep conviction that he had hurdled the second and third conditions of his six-point program. He signaled to the telephone switchboard outside.

"Don't let anybody in and don't put any calls through," he directed. "I'll be busy for the rest of the morning."

When Jackie Robinson left Branch Rickey's office after three of the most amazing hours that he had ever experienced, a whole new world had been opened to his vision. His drooping spirits had been resuscitated as never before. His wildest dream was true.

His head was still whirling, and his ears ringing, but

from a new and more pleasant sound now. He could hear, over and over again, the booming tones of Rickey's repetitious admonition:

"You can't fight back, boy. That's going to be the hardest part of all. No matter what happens, *you can't fight back!*"

Jackie had trouble keeping his feet on the ground. Had trouble avoiding a happy dance-step. He wanted to tell everybody in creation, or somebody, and yet he had been warned by the Brooklyn president to tell nobody.

"But you'll *have* to tell somebody," Rickey had declared. "Or else you'll bust with the news. So tell your mother . . . or your girl, perhaps, but nobody else, mind you!"

He had agreed to accept a bonus of $3500 and a salary of $600 per month. He had agreed to sign a Montreal contract if or when it was proffered to him. And Rickey had promised that it would be offered on or before December 1, 1945. Jackie had agreed to indemnify Rickey against any possible claim that he was under verbal or written contract to anybody.

The monthly salary of $600 was $100 more per month than he was receiving for playing with the Kansas City Monarchs. Straightway he left for California, there to wait until he was summoned by the Brooklyn organization for the next step in the historic move toward entering organized baseball. But would the "impossible" actually happen?

While Branch Rickey had planned to consummate the Jackie Robinson deal by December 1, he had hoped to keep the situation dormant longer than that. If possible, he wanted to postpone actual signing of the player until after the first of the year and use it as rich fodder for the baseball writers.

But the forces of social justice were rampant over the nation. The President's controversial Commission on Fair Employment Practices was already creating havoc in the Southern states. Similar action was concentrated in New York State, and particularly in New York City where percolation was steadily accelerating.

Mayor LaGuardia's sub-committee of his Anti-Discrimination Committee was formed. It was an impressive panel, consisting of ten outstanding men in the field of sports, entertainment, education and politics. They were:

Larry MacPhail, president of the New York Yankees; Branch Rickey, president of the Brooklyn Dodgers; Judge Jeremiah T. Mahoney, former president of the Amateur Athletic Union and political leader; Daniel E. Higgins, of the Board of Education; Edward Lazansky, former presiding judge of the Appellate Division; Dr. J. H. Hudson, Negro sociologist; Arthur Daley, New York *Times* sports columnist; Charles S. Colden, of the Supreme Court of New York State; Prof. Robert M. Haig, Columbia University, and the late Bill Robinson, Negro entertainer. Dr. Dan Dodson, outstanding sociologist and professor at New York University, was secretary of the sub-committee.

The purpose of the group was to work out a practical means of integrating the Negro into organized baseball, not by declaration, but by peaceful solution. The committee agreed that such integration was inevitable and began discussions.

Larry MacPhail, being a spokesman for the American League within the committee, naturally took direct action in formulating policy or leading discussions. He was also, however, a beneficiary of Negro baseball as it was played at the time. President of the New York Yankees and one-third owner of the spacious Yankee Stadium, his club benefitted to the extent of $100,000 annually from rentals to the Negro teams for the large championship games in New York, Newark and Kansas City. Concession sales, programs, etc., of which the tenant received no part, added to the annual take from Negro baseball.

With the interests of his two partners at stake in determining the fate of this considerable income, it was a difficult task for MacPhail or anybody else in the same circumstances to harbor an objective viewpoint in discussing or considering any change in the profitable status of Negro baseball.

So, the Mayor's sub-committee, conceived by a shrewd vote-seeking politician, was headed by two astute baseball club presidents, one hoping for a *status quo* in Negro baseball, and the other with the outstanding Negro player already in his hip pocket as an historic surprise for the public and his unsuspecting associates!

Rickey could hardly expose his secret, which had already cost his organization $25,000 in scouting expense. Yet, he could scarcely take an active part in the discussion of the Negro baseball situation, and suffer the compromise that would result from sitting quietly by and letting MacPhail build up an enormous argument for helping Negro baseball by the simple process of letting it alone.

Presently Rickey solved the situation as it grew hotter by resigning from the Mayor's sub-committee.

This resignation did not deter MacPhail in his avowed plan to get out a report of some kind, of any kind, in the name of the committee, so long as it favored doing little or nothing about the Negro baseball situation. And so, without the authority of the sub-committee as a whole, MacPhail issued a premature report which challenged the existing Negro leagues to "get their house in order," and then to apply for admission to organized baseball. MacPhail said nothing about, nor did the report mention, relief for Negro baseball from the heavy guarantees or rentals to the operators and owners of big-league baseball parks; nor from the 15% exacted by the booking agents. It merely issued a "doubledare" to the Negro leagues, challenging them to lift themselves by their bootstraps.

Several members of the Mayor's sub-committee not only failed to concur, but openly denounced the premature report. Sports writer Arthur Daley was particularly resentful over the steam-roller methods and expressed sharp disagreement with the contents of the MacPhaillian paper.

And for excellent reason, inasmuch as the sub-committee was studying a "Tentative Proposal for Report" which was submitted to each member by Secretary Dodson "purely as a basis for discussion." As handed to Mayor LaGuardia, it outlined the peculiar structure of organized baseball, and then tackled the difficult situation from several angles. Herewith are a few pertinent excerpts from the report "submitted for discussion only" on September 28, 1945:

In contrast to this (organized baseball) there are four Negro leagues. These are loosely organized and it would be difficult to say that they operate with any proximity to the quality of discipline and training achieved in white organized baseball. They constitute at best an opportunity for about four hundred players annually to participate in baseball.

In addition, these Negro teams in the four leagues have a difficult time maintaining schedules which represent a semblance of the professional standard demonstrated in the white leagues. Most of their games are "demonstration games" and most often they play only at the times when they can secure the parks used by the major league teams.

This makes it difficult for Negro boys to get the sort of training necessary for qualification for national recognition in this sport.

Under the heading of "Equity of Negro Baseball," the report for discussion said in part:

The Committee could not overlook the equity of the vested interests which Negroes have in their own leagues. It is estimated that they do a $2,000,000 a year business and the New York Yankee management point out that last year, Negro teams paid $100,000 in rentals and concessions for their four parks in New York, Kansas City, Newark and Norfolk.

These rights cannot be overlooked and yet any major social reform must inevitably run up against such vested interests. It has been pointed out that organized Negro baseball would not have been necessary had Negroes been integrated into the system the same as other minority groups.

It has been pointed out by those in the profession that the Negro players are under contract or reservation to clubs in Negro leagues and that this contractual relationship could not be violated and that the signing of the better Negro players in the major leagues would destroy the interest of Negro teams.

This problem has not been overlooked by the Committee in examining the entire field.

Discussing "Difficulties of Integration," the sub-committee agreed as follows:

1. An analysis of the birthplace of the players in major league baseball reveals the fact that approximately 35% come from states where there is traditional prejudice against Negroes.

   This creates a considerable difficulty in integrating Negroes into the profession. For after all, there is scarcely a field of competition in which tempers are so easily frayed as that of baseball. It is not an uncommon occurrence under the strictest discipline to have two or three fights per season among major league players at the present. The possibilities of this sort of incident, where a Negro player slides into second base and spikes a Southern white boy or vice versa is, of course, a problem to take into account.
2. The problem of spring training is another difficulty to be overcome. Most training is done either in Florida or Cuba. Florida is traditional in its prejudice and, no doubt, if a Negro player accompanied a team to the swanky hotels, he would not be accommodated. This, the Negro player must take into account and must make allowances for in facing his responsibility.

   It is not at all certain that the teams would be welcome at the better hotels in border state cities of Washington, D. C., Cincinnati and St. Louis where the teams are usually accommodated, if they carried on their roster Negro players. If they were not, the Negro would have to understand and make his adjustments to it.
3. Team-work. After all, baseball involves the highest degree of co-operative team performance. The question is raised as to whether or not this could be secured and morale could be maintained if a Negro were a member of the team.

   However, the war experience has shown that where management took a firm stand and went about a process of integration correctly, very few problems resulted. In New York City, in all the ways in which Negroes were integrated into industry and many of them worked alongside whites with Southern background, not a single hate strike was certified to the War Labor Board.

   It would be a sad commentary, both on the part of management and the teams if organized baseball, which allegedly holds to the highest ideals of sportmanship of any sport in the country, cannot approximate this performance of labor.

4. Difficulty of Attracting the New Players. The leadership in the baseball profession has experienced some concern regarding the ability to attract new players. Southern boys, who are being sought both by teams who practice prejudice and those which do not practice discrimination, might prefer to go with the Jim Crow team than the other.

This consideration is no doubt a valid one. On the other hand, the three teams in New York City are in strategic position to offer other inducements which more than cancel such difficulties. One of these is the greater amount of salary which is paid. Two teams in New York City passed the million mark in gate receipts and the third would have, had not a phenomenal long run of week-end games been rained out. Furthermore, so much of the national publicity centers around the teams in New York City, that the prestige of playing on these teams, in our opinion, more than cancels out the difficulties involved.

5. The next of these difficulties is that of reprisals on the part of other clubs of the baseball leagues. These organizations will have to remember that the three teams in New York City are "on the spot." First, because of the legislation and second because of the fact that these clubs will have a difficult time maintaining amicable public relations unless they can conform to public opinion.

It is also doubtful inasmuch as all the major league teams are outside of the Southern part of the United States, if any of these teams can long maintain their present policies of racial segregation. If sportsmanship is to be maintained in the great American tradition, it is inevitable that this bottleneck, whereby 10% of the population of the United States are forbidden the right of competition, must go.

Three pertinent paragraphs from the discussion of the Negro in baseball and Public Opinion are particularly interesting:

While the three New York teams cannot be singled out from the remainder of the country inasmuch a they maintain scheduled games and conduct spring training in the remainder of the country, the New York teams are in the choice position to undertake this pattern of integration due to the fact that public opinion in New York so solidly supports democracy in all activities.

Be the legal aspects as they may, the people of the State of New York set forth their ideals in support of the equality of opportunity and would be unwilling to see their favorite pastime made an exception.

There is little doubt that New York City's baseball public would certainly support the integration of Negroes on the bases of their abilities.

The remainder of the report submitted to Mayor LaGuardia follows in detail:

RECOMMENDATIONS

After careful consideration of these problems, the Committee wishes to make the following recommendations:

1. That Organized Baseball undertake in their proposed postwar expansion, the organization in Southern communities of B, C and/or D minor leagues among Negroes as well as among whites and that in Northern communities adopt immediately a principle of complete integration of Negroes as well as the other minorities at the levels at which their abilities qualify them.

   This should be no handicap in the major portion of the United States and baseball cannot neglect its responsibility for this development.
2. That the Negro baseball leagues be admitted into the field of organized baseball and come under the baseball commissioner's jurisdiction and play under the same standards as those developed in the remainder of the baseball field and that their leagues be classified at whatever level their quality of performance allows whether it be AA or D.
3. Furthermore, we recommend that these Negro leagues, which will no doubt continue to service a unique demand in the Negro community, be given special consideration by the major league clubs operating in the largest cities both in regard to cooperation in scheduling of games and with regard to rentals and concessions in their stadia.

   There is much criticism of the exploitation of the Negro teams by the concessionaires and managers of parks and furthermore, we recommend that contractual relations be established with these clubs on a basis comparable to that arranged between clubs within the major and minor leagues.

   If it is profitable for the "Yankees" to own a white club in Newark, it should likewise be profitable for them to own a Negro club in New York City or elsewhere or, failing of this relationship, certainly contractual agreements could be developed such as those existing between the "Dodgers" and St. Paul, Mobile, Burlington and Zanesville.

In this fashion, the contractual relationships between club managers of Negroes and major league teams could be adequately handled.

4. We recommend that simultaneously with, but not dependent upon, this organizational set up, the New York clubs integrate Negroes at whatever level their abilities merit both in major league clubs and in farm systems—keeping in mind the recommendation made in #1 above.

Certainly, in "Dodger," "Yankee" and "Giant" farms in the International League, Negro players who might qualify for experience in this league could be used without difficulty.

The same would perhaps be true with any clubs of the Pacific Coast and no doubt with the major clubs of the American Association except Louisville. Once this set up is achieved, there should be no difficulty of promotion of Negroes within the system. Any antipathies existing between groups would soon be overcome for organized baseball the United States over, because of the fact that Southern white players, in acquiring their experience in the minor leagues, would have included in that experience that of playing with and against Negro players.

IN CONCLUSION

There was never a more propitious moment than the present, when we are just concluding a terrible World War to suppress the theory of racial superiority, to put our own house in order.

The Committee is not asking that major league baseball inject the race issue to the extent of lowering of its standards. No one demands that Negroes be integrated at levels above their abilities.

This would be the last desire of any member of this Committee. The Committee does believe that organized baseball owes the same responsibility to the community as does every other sport, business or industry to make sure that this vicious pattern of race segregation is eliminated.

CHAPTER 9

THE CONFLICT between the premature MacPhail report and the sub-committee's official treatise "for discussion only" threw the Negro situation into sharper focus in Metropolitan New York City. At no time did the panel of ten as a body regard the four Negro leagues as needing anything but maximum help and understanding in order to be a part of the national game.

But this was only the beginning of the furore which seemed to accelerate as the November Election Day moved closer. The Negro and baseball was a popular vehicle with all political parties.

Governor Dewey's Ives-Quinn Law Committee of five descended upon New York City in late September without warning. They called upon the three presidents of the major league baseball clubs operating in New York City to appear for an important discussion relating to social justice. Rickey, MacPhail and Horace Stoneham, of the Giants, appeared, but Stoneham brought Edgar P. Feeley, his club attorney and vice president.

The committee from Albany, consisting of four men and a woman, squandered little breath in discussing the intangibles of the situation. Time was a-wasting, and the State's position among racial groups had to be proclaimed as well as fortified. This fortification took the form of a sheet of paper on which were two brief, typewritten paragraphs. It was, in effect, a pledge which the three club presidents would sign, binding them to frank declaration that they would not discriminate on the basis of race, color or creed in the hiring or firing of employees within the Empire State.

For once Larry MacPhail's explosive nature was beaten to the fuse. It was Horace Stoneham whose dudgeon reached a new altitude when he hit the ceiling with such force, figuratively, of course, that he had to be lifted down in pieces. Stoneham effervesced in all directions, and was an emphatic spokesman for the three big league clubs in denouncing the Albany committee, individually and collectively, for daring to force the issue in such a manner. He termed it a coercive effort in the field of racial and religious relations which his New York Giants had always solved and would continue to solve without signed pledges, before or after election!

As a result, the Ives-Quinn committee members returned to Governor Dewey without signed ammunition for the forthcoming issues at the polls. The Negro vote was still at large for whoever could make the deepest impression on it.

While the activities of the Mayor's sub-committee and the Governor's quintet were more or less secret, those of communistic Councilman Ben Davis were not. He was openly attacking organized baseball on street corners and seeking to capitalize on his unusual sports background as a great football player for Amherst College. He pledged wildly that he would force baseball to open its doors to members of his race.

Meanwhile, Mayor LaGuardia was heightening his own actions through the medium of his Sunday radio broadcast. He had built up a considerable following through an assortment of specialized wisdom and opinions, which included advice to the lovelorn, cooking recipes, hints to the newly married, reading of the Sunday comics, particularly during newspaper strikes, and anything that would capture listening fancy. Now he saw the Negro baseball situation as an ideal springboard into the deep water. Why couldn't his sub-committee be the instrument by which the Mayor could be seen as forcing baseball to accept and hire Negroes?

No reason why this wasn't possible, except that a couple of his sub-committee members didn't like the idea of using the situation as a political vehicle. One was the committee secretary, Dr. Dodson. The other was Judge Lazansky. The elderly judge, always a humanitarian, was particularly distressed over the way the Mayor's laudable project had been diverted to political use. And so, one evening at a Brooklyn hotel function, he drew Branch Rickey aside and whispered in a hesitant voice:

"I feel I must tell you, Branch. Our committee's an election football!"

Rickey was now faced with a bigger problem than

ever. He did not have his Negro player under contract. He merely had an understanding, a meeting of the minds. He had so timed his moves as to make it a midwinter revelation, rather than a hurried accomplishment. But the forces of politics and the wolves of social justice were barking at his heels. It is possible that a few people guessed or even surmised what he had done.

Whether or not, in mid-October the Mayor made a specific request of Rickey, through Dr. Dodson, to let him, LaGuardia, announce over his radio program that "baseball would shortly begin signing Negro players, and that it was the direct result of the Mayor's Committee on Anti-Discrimination." This he wished for a forthcoming Sunday broadcast (October 21) and he assumed that the favor would be granted without further discussion.

However, Branch Rickey sent word back through Dr. Dodson that he would like another week, and would the Mayor please postpone the scheduled broadcast? LaGuardia readily consented and used a substitute program.

Rickey then wired Robinson to proceed East and fly directly to Montreal. There, on the afternoon of Tuesday, October 23, 1945, Jackie Robinson signed a contract to play for the Montreal Royals in the offices of Hector Racine, club president. Looking on were Branch Rickey, Jr., then Director of Minor League teams for the Brooklyn organization; and Col. Romeo Gauvreau, vice-president of the Royals. Through that signing, the news was given to the country and the world at large without any political, racial, or religious identification. Robinson was signed as a baseball player who hoped to make good on skill alone.

With that the dam burst. Rickey and Robinson were marked men.

The first official protest against the signing was registered before midnight. It came from T. Y. Baird, co-owner of the Kansas City Monarchs. In an Associated Press dispatch he declared that he would appeal to the new baseball Commissioner, A. B. Chandler. He was quoted as saying:

"Robinson signed a contract with us last year and I feel that he is our property. If Chandler lets Montreal and Brooklyn get by with that, he is really starting a mess."

The venerable Clark Griffith, part-owner of the Washington Senators and whose Stadium was the scene of many big Negro baseball games in the course of a year, declared, "The only question that occurs to me is whether organized baseball has a right to sign a player from the Negro league. That is a well-established league and organized baseball shouldn't take their players. The Negro league is entitled to full recognition as a full-fledged baseball organization."

In reply to this, Branch Rickey said on Oct. 25; "There is no Negro league as such as far as I am concerned. Negro baseball is in the zone of a racket and there is not a circuit that could be admitted to organized baseball, Clark Griffith of Washington to the contrary."

And then from distant points came hastily arranged

comments which are interesting to review at this time.

The late W. G. Bramham, commissioner of minor league baseball, contributed the following gem: "Father Divine will have to look to his laurels, for we can expect Rickey Temple to be in the course of construction in Harlem soon."

Bramham augmented this half-witticism two days later with a more sober expostulation, to wit: "It is those of the carpet-bagger stripe of the white race, under the guise of helping, but in truth using the Negro for their own selfish ends, who retard the race.

"It is my opinion that if the Negro is left alone and aided by his own unselfish friends of the white race, he will work out his own salvation in all lines of endeavor. Whenever I hear a white man, whether he be from the North, South, East or West, broadcasting what a Moses he is to the Negro race, right then I know that the latter needs a body-guard."

Three days after his intemperate outburst, T. Y. Baird, of the Kansas City Monarchs, telegraphed Rickey, "Sorry my interview with the Associated Press relative to Jackie Robinson misquoted also misinterpreted. Would not do anything to hamper or impede the advancement of any Negro ball player, nor would we do anything to keep any Negro ball player out of white major leagues." And his partner, J. L. Wilkinson, concurred in the same manner. Both owners, it might be noted, are white men.

Bob Feller, of the Cleveland Indians, having pitched three times to Jackie Robinson in a recent exhibition game on the Pacific Coast, felt qualified to offer the following critique: "Good field—no hit. Sucker for an inside pitch." A few days later Feller enlarged the statement with, "Jackie will be in a tough spot. I'm not prejudiced against him, either. I hope he makes good, but, frankly, I don't think he will."

Dan Daniel, one of the country's most respected and widely read baseball authorities as staff writer for the New York *World Telegram* and *The Sun*, wrote in the *Sporting News:*

"It is quite conceivable that the story has received far more attention than it is worth.

"Robinson has not been signed by the Dodgers, and insofar as can be discerned, never will play for the Brooklyn club in the National League."

From Durham, N. C., headquarters of minor league baseball, came two conflicting statements from the typewriters of rival sports writers. Jack Horner, of the *Morning Herald*, who quoted Judge Bramham so glibly, closed with his own opinion as follows:

"The general impression in this southern city is that the Negro player will be so uncomfortable, embarrassed and out of place in organized baseball, that he will soon get out of his own accord."

Exception to the above 'general impression' was the expressed observation of Hugh Germinio in the Durham *Sun*, to wit:

"If a colored player is good enough to make the major leagues, then I want to see him have that opportunity."

Eddie Collins, then vice-president and general manager of the Boston Red Sox, made a startling revelation about existing opportunity for Negroes in minor league baseball when he was quoted as saying:

"Jackie Robinson worked out for us last Spring. Very few players can step into the majors from college or sandlot ball. Of course, they always have the chance to prove themselves in the minors. (*Sic*) More power to Robinson if he can make the grade."

The minor league opportunities referred to by Collins obviously relate to two Negroes, Stovey and Walker, who played at Newark, N. J., before the turn of the century, and that some twenty Negroes were reported playing minor league baseball in 1887. It is a matter of record that organized baseball had never admitted more than a sun-tanned Cuban in sixty years of social progress.

Dick McCann, then sports writer for the Washington *Times-Herald*, who became the first director of the professional Football Hall of Fame, disputed the claim that Robinson would be the victim of poor sportsmanship when he wrote:

"We don't agree with those who think that other major league ball players will resent Jackie Robinson and others of his race, if and when, they make the grade. Your American athlete is, essentially, a good sport . . . far fairer than even the American fan."

W. N. Cox, of the Norfolk (Va.) *Virginian Pilot*, x-rayed the smoke screen of pride and prejudice and saw the real issue:

"The mainspring in this question," he wrote, "is the Negro ball player's ability to deliver on the line in competition. I guarantee that if Jackie Robinson hits homers and plays a whale of a game for Montreal, the fans will soon lose sight of his color."

Rogers Hornsby, one of Rickey's baseball immortals, when questioned, said:

"The way things are, it will be tough for a Negro player to become part of a close-knit group such as an organized ball club. I think Branch Rickey was wrong in signing Robinson to play with Montreal, and that it won't work out."

From Birmingham, Ala., came the crisp comment of Brooklyn's most popular player, outfielder Dixie Walker: "As long as he isn't with the Dodgers, I'm not worried."

The St. Louis *Sporting News*, popularly known as "the Bible of Baseball," digested sports page comment from thousands of newspapers, and then offered its disciples the following Gospel:

"Robinson, at 26, is reported to possess baseball abilities which, were he white, would make him eligible for a trial with, let us say, the Brooklyn Dodgers' Class B farm at Newport News, if he were six years younger.

"He is thrown into the post-war reconstruction of baseball, and placed in competition with a vast number of younger, more skilled and more experienced players. . . . This factor alone appears likely to beat him down."

That week's baseball Scripture also contained the expressed belief that the attention which the signing of Robinson elicited in the press around the country was out of proportion to the actual vitality of the story.

But on the whole, newspaper opinion and interpretation was more objective. Editorial pages were consistently favorable to the surprising incursion of the Negro player.

However, Branch Rickey's prime purpose, oft expressed, seemed to be lost in the interpretive shuffle. It was variously called the result of political pressure, box-office novelty, a post-war publicity stunt, etc. Virtually no one seemed to believe that he merely wanted a baseball player and firmly believed that he had signed one in Jackie Robinson.

CHAPTER 10

THERE WAS much speculation as to whether Robinson would be Rickey's only Negro player, or the spearhead of a general influx. In answer to questions, the Dodger president declared that he had "looked at many and might sign more." Regardless, the majority believed that he would use Jackie as a guinea pig for a season and regulate future actions by the single experiment.

Those who regarded Robinson as Rickey's only colored candidate were amazed some weeks later when he announced the signing of four more Negro baseball players: John Wright, a pitcher; Don Newcombe, a pitcher; Roy Campanella, a catcher; and Roy Partlow, a left-handed pitcher. They were signed in that order.

Few people today realize the effective enormity of Rickey's scouting program during 1943–44–45, and the results obtained. Of these five Negro "firsts," Robinson's status is assured as one of the great names in Dodger history and one of the greatest box office draws since Babe Ruth. Roy Campanella is acknowledged everywhere to have been one of the finest catchers baseball ever saw. Don Newcombe, Rookie of the Year in 1949, became one of Brooklyn's biggest winners and most talked about stars. Wright failed, and Partlow, being 37 years old at the time of signing, was not expected to go very far. This is what Rickey paid them:

Player	Cash Bonus	Monthly Salary
Robinson	$3500	$600
Wright	3250	350
Newcombe	1000	350
*Campanella	2900	185
**Partlow	2500	400
	$13,150	$1885

*Includes $500 for special work after season.

**Includes $1000 paid to Philadelphia Stars after learning that Partlow had verbal agreement to sign with them for 1946.

Through the Winter months it was obvious that Branch Rickey had caught the field flat-footed. He had outsmarted the politicians, and he had circumvented the stand-patters of organized baseball, and he had dealt a devastating blow at the so-called Negro leagues.

It was a bitter pill for organized baseball to swallow, and some of the executives in council simply refused to take it lying down or otherwise. This recalcitrance was expressed in December, 1945 by an amazing declaration within a report which read, ". . . however well-intentioned, the use of Negro players (in the big leagues) would hazard all the physical properties of baseball."

Robinson had not even played a game of organized baseball, yet here was a denouncement, which seven other National League club owners were reading without protest and turning back to their president, Ford Frick, who polled all to make sure they knew of the contents. He then carefully checked the names on the reports to see that all copies had been returned.

Rickey sat spellbound in the joint meeting of both American and National Leagues next day as this formal disapproval was railroaded through to acceptance as part of a report which also contained sharp criticism of the new Commissioner, Chandler. Not a voice of protest was raised, unfortunately not even his own, Rickey learned later.

For two years Rickey rankled over the memory of this un-American declaration, adopted in the most un-American fashion by a sport that is supposed to reflect the very principles of American democracy. He spoke of it on more than one occasion, and always wound up heaving away a half-smoked cigar to alleviate his feeling of disgust. He shuddered at what would happen publicity-wise, had word of the pussy-footing legislation leaked out. When Rickey tried to obtain a copy, he was told that they had been destroyed.

Rickey finally publicized the story in what was to be an innocuous speech before Wilberforce College at Wilberforce, O., on Feb. 16, 1948. He used the tale ostensibly to illustrate how people's objection to change is usually based more on ignorance of the outcome, rather than fear. He cited the number of clubs that were scouting and signing Negroes at the time, which was in marked contrast to the declaration approved by the big leagues in joint session only two years before.

But the speech brought an avalanche of criticism upon Rickey's head. Larry MacPhail, who had sold his New York Yankee interests to his wealthy partners suddenly at the end of the 1947 season, emerged from vocal retirement in Miami Beach to heap a tirade of abuse upon his former benefactor. In a 1000-word statement, he called Rickey a liar four times, but each time carefully qualified the excoriation with "if and when he said." Inasmuch as Rickey had never said any of the things on which MacPhail's disparagement was based, the expostulation was no more than a characteristic cascade of wind.

The colorful redhead used the situation as a means of venting his chagrin. But in order to do so, he had to play fast and loose with facts, for the United Press quoted him as saying:

"This report (his premature paper that had outraged the subcommittee) was published before Rickey signed Robinson to a contract calling for less money than Robinson made in the Negro leagues."

Rickey studied the verbiage credited to MacPhail, but

nowhere could he find a denial of his Wilberforce statement that expressed disapproval of Negroes in baseball was part of a report adopted formally by club owners. No executive in baseball denied it in the welter of quotations and misquotations that followed. No one, not even MacPhail, denied that copies of the adopted report had been confiscated.

Instead, Rickey was generally charged with stirring up racial bias and seeking publicity. The noise of the clubs beating against the well-pounded Rickey skull drowned his cries of protest.

His comment on MacPhail's verbal fireworks in Miami was terse. Having started Larry in baseball at Columbus, Ohio, having helped him land a job with the Cincinnati Reds, and having been responsible for getting him the general management job with the Brooklyn Dodgers in 1937, Rickey understood everything that MacPhail did or said, true or false. And so, of the 1000-word dispatch from Miami, he said:

"That is a typical MacPhaillian outburst. I would have been disappointed with anything else."

The presence of Negroes in organized baseball during the winter of 1945–46 was grist indeed for the typewriting mills. A writer could scarcely take a middle road, for the fans wanted no middle road. In order to attract attention, the sports writer, particularly the columnist, took a positive stand and began to interpret all ramifications of the development. Little could be gained by heralding Rickey as a Moses, or the starter of constructive moves. This would be a reflection upon other owners who somehow hadn't got around to doing the same thing first.

The alternative was to attack Rickey's motives, his sincerity, his integrity and even his methods. His repetitious insistence that he was after good ball players and believed he had them was ridiculed. All you had to do to attract attention in the mass circulation field was knock Rickey's brains out in print. And a small regiment of these forces began a determined tattoo.

The most unequivocal denunciation of Branch Rickey appeared in the "Powerhouse" column of the New York *Daily News* on March 12, 1946, presumably written by Jimmy Powers, the sports editor. His long-range prophecy for 2,500,000 readers that day was:

"We wrote before and we repeat it here that we don't believe Jackie Robinson, colored college star signed by the Dodgers for one of their farm teams, will ever play in the big leagues. We question Branch Rickey's pompous statements that he is another Abraham Lincoln and that he has a heart as big as a watermelon and he loves all mankind."

This statement, the heart of the column, became a matter of government concern shortly after when Dr. John J. Johnson, chairman of the Mayor's Committee on Baseball, used the municipal radio station, WNYC, as a means of striking back at Powers with a condemnatory broadcast which said in part ". . . the article casts aspersion and hurls insults upon those who are trying to improve interfaith and interracial relations by suggestion and innuendo, by false premises and by statements that are directly untrue, and it can have no other effect than to stir up fears, suspicions and hatreds between people of different races."

The Federal Communications Commission looked into the matter after attorneys for the *Daily News* had protested against reading such scurrilous matter over a city-owned radio station. Dr. Dan Dodson, executive director of the Mayor's Committee on Baseball, was called before the FCC under threat of subpoena to identify Dr. Johnson's news release based on the Powerhouse article. He not only identified it, but supported the Johnson stand. Answering the challenge of *Daily News* attorneys, Dr. Dodson called the Powers attack a deliberate attempt to discredit Branch Rickey and his efforts to integrate the Negro into baseball.

Inasmuch as the Mayor's Committee made no retraction, and suffered no official reprimand, or warning about future radio reprisals of this nature, the Powerhouse position remained condemned and the FCC acknowledged the right of free speech.

Meanwhile, Jackie Robinson was making the rest of his dream come true. He took part in a baseball barnstorming trip to South America, and then claimed his bride, Rachel Isum, in Los Angeles.

It is quite possible that the happiest day of Mallie McGriff Robinson's life was February 10, 1946, though she has experienced many pleasant days since. But on this day her youngest child was marrying the girl she considered the very best of all. He had earned what to her was a small fortune through his persistent love of athletics and games. And there he was, dressed in starched linens, gleaming cutaway coat and striped trousers.

And there was Rae Isum, beautiful as any bride could be, dressed in long veil and crown, glistening white satin and carrying native orange blossoms.

But best of all, there was the Rev. Karl Downs, the personification of God's goodness and charity on earth; the disciple of Christ who had comforted her through more troublesome hours than a human is supposed to endure. How many years had Rev. Downs been at Scott's Methodist Church? Mallie Robinson had forgotten. All she knew was that he had flown by airplane from Sam Houston College, at Austin, Texas, just to perform this marriage ceremony for the baby of her family.

It had been a long, rough journey from Cairo, Georgia, to this, more than a quarter century later. Mallie Robinson treasured every hour, the good and the bad, but this hour she treasured above all.

For her Jackie hadn't forgotten to remember kindnesses, which explained the presence of Babe Horrell, his old football coach, and the indefatigable Lippy Duckat.

CHAPTER 11

THE BIG TEST of the Negro baseball situation was not in the printed word. Rickey had maintained that the great problem would come at Daytona Beach and other Florida towns where Brooklyn and Montreal were scheduled to play during the 1946 training season. To obviate difficulty and misunderstanding, he dispatched his then presidential assistant, Bob Finch, to Daytona Beach shortly after the first of the year for the purpose of locating Robinson and his bride, and the second Negro with the Montreal team, pitcher John Wright. All municipal regulations relating to permission or prohibition in the matter of colored athletes were examined. Neither Brooklyn nor Montreal was to violate any existing codes of conduct.

Finch arranged to have the Robinsons and Wright quartered at the home of E. B. Brock, a well-to-do Florida Negro. The two players were to don uniforms at the house. Montreal would be part of an augmented minor league camp at Sanford, the forerunner of the present Vero Beach training extravaganza, which has been adopted by several big league clubs for their farm teams. Brooklyn, of course, would be installed at Daytona Beach.

Not the least of Rickey's concerns was his Montreal manager, Clay Hopper, a respected citizen of Greenwood, Mississippi. Hopper had been lifted by Rickey from Class B management and installed in Triple-A company at Montreal. There Hopper had shown unusual skill in developing high-classification minor league rookies, the foundation of Brooklyn's hopes for future pennants.

Hopper's position, therefore, was of great importance. Loyalty to Rickey was one thing, but the presentation of organized baseball's first Negro player for handling and developing, was something else again, especially to a respected citizen of Greenwood, Mississippi. Hopper had taken the news of Robinson's signing with discreet and stoical silence. Now at Sanford and Daytona Beach, he viewed the player for the first time.

Not even Branch Rickey realized the depth of the problem to Clay Hopper. His unruffled demeanor gave no hint of the turmoil that must have tried his southern soul. He performed the training camp functions, attended to his players and there is no record of bad manners or outward sign of antipathy toward Robinson or Wright.

Not until the man from Mississippi was seated next to Rickey one day during a game at Daytona Beach did Hopper weaken. They were watching Robinson star in an intersquad contest, and he had felt Rickey's enthusiastic elbow several times in his ribs as Robinson went far afield for ground balls. The fourth and hardest jab punctuated a near-fantastic fielding gem by the Negro, whereupon Hopper whirled about and grabbed Rickey's coat lapels in his clenched fists. With his narrowed eyes close to Rickey's, he exclaimed with deepest emotion:

"Mistuh Rickey, do you *really* think a nigger's a human bein'?"

Rickey's first impulse was to laugh, not in humor, but to relieve the unexpected tension. But as Hopper's grip relaxed and he turned his gray head away, the embarrassment eased. Rickey said nothing, but he awakened to the fact that his Montreal manager was indeed carrying a greater emotional load than anyone had suspected. For many weeks Rickey wondered if Hopper would be able to complete the job without incident or nervous breakdown.

The itinerant reporters pounced upon Rickey at every opportunity, for statements, because the Robinson-Wright situation at Daytona was the hottest thing since the invention of tabasco sauce.

"I can only repeat, gentlemen," Rickey said once more, "that my desire to build a championship team for Brooklyn is intense. If an elephant with pink ears were a better center fielder for the Dodgers than the best player the team had for that position, I would sign the elephant to a contract and put him in center field."

One of Jackie's toughest jobs during training was to "learn" organized baseball. He found it an education in itself when Paul Chervinko and Clyde Sukeforth, both former catchers, went to work on him with hit signs, established procedure, when to put on the hit-and-run, and when it shouldn't be put on, breaks and leads off the bags to capitalize on his base-running power.

"It was my biggest trouble," Jackie declared. "Nobody ever before told me the correct way to do things in baseball."

One of the welcome sights to him was the appearance of Bob Daley, an outfielder, on the Montreal squad. Here was a friendly face who had played many baseball games with him at Atascadero. Daley proved a friend indeed by talking about Jackie to newspapermen, telling of his California background, NYA work and personality—things that Jackie couldn't tell about himself.

The most unwelcome sight was one Señor R. Janis, of Laredo, Texas, who had the audacity to offer Jackie $6000 per season and all expenses to play baseball for the Pasquel brothers in Mexico.

"I wouldn't accept," Jackie laughed, "if they gave me the five hundred thousand dollars they offered Ted Williams."

Branch Rickey chased Señor Janis hither and yon, finally cornering and catching him at nearby City Island Park. He shouted:

"Don't you know these men are under contract?"

"Are they?" the señor echoed blandly.

The Dodger president gave him the heave-ho, but the persistent señor registered at the New Gables Hotel under various aliases—J. Roberts, R. Jaminez, R. Jaggy, etc. The unwelcome visitor clouded the otherwise bright situation, and finally bagged a few of the Montreal players who disappeared into Mexican baseball.

Rickey's hopes for an uneventful training season for the Negro players were further blasted in mid-March, when Montreal appeared in Jacksonville for an exhibition game with the Jersey City Giants. Although clearance had been promised by authorities, executive secretary of the Jacksonville playgrounds, George Robinson, said that the by-laws of the city constitution forbade competition among whites and coloreds on city-owned grounds. Forthwith, the team climbed into the bus and, with Robinson still in their midst, returned to training camp without playing a game at all.

A second game, scheduled with Indianapolis at DeLand, Fla., was held up when Montreal arrived, and the explanation was that lights were being fixed. Asked just what the lights had to do with a daytime game, authorities replied that the electricians were available only on that day, and that the teams couldn't use the field.

It was obvious, of course, that executives of the Florida municipalities were reluctant to make history in the field of mixed competition. When games were cancelled at Savannah, Ga., and Richmond, Va., on the way North, it meant that Montreal would have to train out of the country in the future, if games were to be played, and that Brooklyn would be obliged to plan likewise, should its roster contain any Negroes. It also heralded added training costs, the flying of players over ocean, and incurring the wrath of pro-Florida baseball writers assigned to the Dodgers. And yet, at no time did Branch Rickey indicate a willingness to give Robinson anything but a thorough trial in organized baseball.

An interesting contrast to the Hopper predicament was presented by Frank Shaughnessy, president of the International League, who was faced with the responsibility to social justice on one hand, and the protection of the club owners' capital investment in his league and public safety on the other. Shaughnessy, a red-faced, strapping former player, had risen from the ranks of athletic skill to high places of baseball administration, the latter partly through the guidance of Branch Rickey.

The league president admired Rickey as a friend and pillar of baseball, but he finally succumbed to the pressure as presented by what seemed to be a cross section of feeling in Baltimore and expressed in the lurid headlines of the daily papers. Shaughnessy carried clippings from the papers as he waited in the anteroom of Rickey's office early one April morning in 1946. He rose quickly from his chair as Rickey entered.

"I've been here since eight-thirty, Branch," he said. "I'm worried."

"Been up since five o'clock myself," Rickey replied and motioned for him to follow into the inner office. "Big day for everybody . . . trouble ahead, trouble ahead. Nobody can see anything but trouble."

"But Branch, there *is* trouble ahead—"

"That's what old Mrs. Overbrook said on her first train ride," Rickey laughed. "Thought for sure the train would disappear right over the cliff. It was her first trip outside of Duck Run—that's in Southern Ohio—but, do you know, just as she was ready for the end of the world, the train skimmed right around a curve and she had the best time of her life. Trouble ahead—"

"Branch!" Shaughnessy exclaimed. "If you knew there would be riots in Baltimore when this boy appeared, that people would be hurt, would you send him down there?"

Rickey's head moved from side to side. "No, I wouldn't."

"If you knew that the presence of this boy in the Municipal Stadium at Baltimore would produce bloodshed, and perhaps end baseball in that city," Shaughnessy exclaimed, "would you let Robinson go there?"

"No, I wouldn't!" Rickey barked.

"Then, for God's sake, don't let him go," the league president pleaded. "Because that's what will happen. They're up in arms. Here are the stories. It's in all the papers. Don't let it happen, Branch."

Rickey examined the clippings. It was all prophesied, if the Negro was allowed to play. He knew that Shaughnessy was not expressing a personal opinion. Rather he was doing what he thought best for his league.

"But I don't think these awful things *will* happen," Rickey declared. "So, Robinson will go to Baltimore with his team!"

Rickey selected a cigar from the humidor and saw Shaughnessy to the door.

"Thanks for your visit," he said. "Meanwhile, I'll see you at Jersey City this afternoon. Let's see if we can find out whether Robinson is worth taking to Baltimore."

It was indeed an epochal day in baseball, April 18, 1946, when Robinson, second base for Montreal, appeared before 25,000 people in Roosevelt Stadium, Jersey City, his first official contest in organized baseball. It is doubtful that any player, working under the pressure that was Robinson's, ever turned in a more thrilling or fortuitous beginning. It opened in very humble fashion. In his first time at bat, he swung at a three-and-two pitch, and grounded out to short. Then he muffed an easy throw for an error on a double play and not only lost both men, but permitted a runner on third to score.

But then the fun began. In his second time at bat, with two Royals on base in the third inning, he drove a ball into the left field bleachers for a home run. In the fifth inning he bunted toward third and beat it out for a hit. He stole second, went to third on an infield out and so tantalized the southpaw, Warren Sandell, that the rookie balked and permitted Robinson to score. He singled cleanly to left in the seventh, stole second and scored on a single. He bunted safely again in the ninth, went to third on a single, and so annoyed the pitcher again that another balk permitted him to score. Montreal won 14 to 1.

Jackie's total for the day was four runs batted in, four runs scored, two stolen bases and two balks. Most of the 25,000 spectators stormed the field after the game, and it took Robinson five minutes to reach the clubhouse.

And while this triumph was in the making, Robinson's bride of a few months, his sweetheart from UCLA college days, was wandering through the large crowd, her ears picking up the assorted comments, threats and intimations. Like a hunted animal, she threaded her way through the aisles, passing as close to the anti-Robinsonites as she dared. Too nervous to occupy her own seat, she was unable to remain quiet until it was all over, when she could meet her man at the clubhouse, take his arm and march away with him. During the terrifying ordeal, she had heard enough to frighten the daylights out of her. If this was the sentiment in Jersey City, she thought, what would it be like in Baltimore?

Results for the opening of the season in Baltimore's Municipal (now Babe Ruth) Stadium on the night of May 27, 1946 were not quite as electrifying as Jackie Robinson had expected. He, too, had been victimized by "trouble ahead" thinking. He had been concerned about Rae, and had even asked her not to make the trip to Maryland. But she accompanied him to a colored hotel.

Immediately Jackie was badgered by sports writers wanting to know whether he would protest the segregation, but he reflected the policy of the Brooklyn organization, which was to settle things on the ball field, and nowhere else.

"Why should I protest?" Jackie replied to questioners. "It's not my business. It's the custom of the city and I respect it."

More than 25,000 fans, many of whom were Negro, turned out for the nocturnal inaugural, and the overwhelming number of jeers when Jackie became the center of action indicated that he was resented. But soon the ball game became more important than any one in it, particularly Robinson. When the Royals forged ahead, they began to jeer the Orioles. When Robinson cracked out a single as an important part of a scoring rally, there were more cheers than jeers. And when he stole his first Baltimore base, the cheering was enthusiastic and overwhelming. At the end of the game, they leaped on to the field and followed him to the distant clubhouse. No incidents, except a close pitch that hit his wrist.

Four days later the second largest crowd ever to see a baseball game in Montreal, 15,745, turned out for the opening of the International League season. Their Royals were in the lead and they wanted to see organized baseball's first Negro player.

Notable is that 66,551 fans had paid to see three opening games in which Jackie took part!

Jackie produced a single in four times at bat to delight the crowd, and thereafter he delighted the Royal fans daily. He played second base as Montreal had never seen it played before. He took part in fifteen double plays within a period of twelve games. He made only two errors in the twenty home games.

On Decoration Day he was leading the league in hitting with an average of .356. Already the rumors were flying, most startling of which was that Branch Rickey planned his transfer to the Dodgers. He was acclaimed as a good player by some, as great by others.

Lloyd McGowan, Montreal sports writer, wrote,

"When the Royals completed their first home stand on May 26, Jackie Robinson was no longer the question mark of the infield. On the contrary, the Branch Rickey protegé is regarded as the Royals' strongest inner guard. And Manager Clay Hopper says that he hasn't seen anybody around the league who can outplay Robinson at second base.

"Of course the road is tough and long and it's the first trip for Jackie in organized baseball. But for the present the grandstand chant for him is 'Glad to have you with us.' "

Despite all this, no roofs had caved in from the shock of a Negro's presence in organized baseball. There had been no riots, except by the more aggressive autograph hounds. The sun was still rising in the East and setting in the West. International League attendance had increased in every city and ticket managers observed that once the money was in the till, you couldn't tell whether it had been paid by a white man or a colored man.

The mainspring, as W. N. Cox had noted in the Norfolk *Virginian Pilot*, was the Negro player's ability to deliver on the line in competition. Baseball fans had become color blind.

It was more than a few disgruntled cared to tolerate, chief of whom was T. Y. Baird, co-owner of the Kansas City Monarchs. He reneged on his telegram to Branch Rickey and put forth a claim for cash on the strength of an alleged verbal contract between the club and Robinson. His cry reached the sympathetic ears of Dan Parker, militant sports editor of the New York *Daily*

Mirror, whose column is always open to a revelation of unfairness in sports. Parker reflected Baird's claim, and publication resulted in depositions from all five Negro players under contract in the Dodger organization. Each player stated unequivocally that he was not under contract. The Robinson statement is offered herein. The others were similar, though not identical.

Dear Mr. Rickey— July 13, 1946

I have just read Mr. Parker's article in the Mirror stating in effect I had violated my contract with the Kansas City Monarchs and that you had induced me to do so. The facts are as follows:

No contract of any kind was ever tendered to me by the Kansas City Monarchs and I had never signed anything in the nature of an agreement or a contract with that club. I simply received an offer in a letter and I reported to the Kansas City Monarchs as a result of that letter.

Upon reporting I asked William Dismukes, the business manager of the Monarchs, for a contract but none was ever tendered to me. I knew that I had no job at any minute they cared to dismiss me. Furthermore, at no time did I have a conversation with anyone connected with the Kansas City Monarchs or with any other club for that matter in regard to my future services.

Some time ago, I read in the press a statement by Mr. Wilkinson, the owner of the Kansas City Monarchs, stating that I was under no contract with his club.

When I came to Brooklyn to see you one of the very first questions you asked me, if not the very first, was "are you under any obligation of any sort whatever as to your future services in baseball?" I told you very quickly "none whatever." You asked me to put that in writing and I did so at that time.

As I remember our first conversation you gave me to understand that if I had any agreement with my then employers you could not discuss my employment by the Brooklyn organization.

Sincerely yours,
/signed/ Jackie Robinson

At the close of the season, Branch Rickey sent photostat copies of all five depositions to Parker and other sports writers, along with a lengthy and detailed explanation of the scouting and signing of the players. Despite this frank and honest effort to clarify the situation, Rickey was badgered from time to time with columnar barbs, such as:

"When is Branch Rickey going to pay the Kansas City Monarchs the $15,000 he owes them for Jackie Robinson?"

But it couldn't stop Jackie Robinson's sensational climb to the top of the International League canopy of stars. Not only was he hitting, he was base-stealing. With fleet Marvin Rackley, an outfielder, on base with Jackie, there was no peace for catchers. Rackley wound up stealing 65 bases and Jackie 40, and speeding from first to third on a bunt was no novelty. In late August Bruno Betzel, Jersey City skipper, said, "He's the best ball player in the league. Better than Ty Cobb as a bunter and the best base-runner in the game!"

Jackie would have captured all the baseball headlines that year but for the Mexican baseball situation. The departure of more than thirty players in violation of the reserve clause in the uniform contract produced a serious situation, particularly in the post-war situation when man power was at a premium to club owners.

But the Negro charged on to a brilliant finish, leading the Montreal Royals to a run-away victory in the regular season and in the Shaughnessy Playoffs. It was a memorable triumph for team and individual as well.

For Jackie Robinson emerged as batting champion of the league with a record of .349, the result of 155 hits in 444 times at bat. He had missed thirty games of the schedule—a full week in June—due to a recurrence of his ankle injury. He had been hit by pitchers a record number of times, but always came back to swing at the good ball. He had led the league in run-scoring, 112. He had led the league's second basemen defensively, making only ten errors in 674 chances for a high percentage of .985.

And now he was going into Louisville, Kentucky, there to be the first Negro ever to play a game with white men. The Colonels were champions of the American Association, and were to meet the Royals for the Little World Series. Jackie himself wondered if he might be pressing his luck too far; wondered if baseball was strong enough to carry this burden. He was still wondering as he went on Parkway Field for the first of three games at Louisville.

The stands were packed with white people. The Jim Crow section was packed with colored fans. Jackie's appearance brought forth a chorus of jeers that drowned out the cheers, if any. The colored folks were happy to see the impossible and most of them cheered silently. They jammed the park, stood outside in the streets and crowded on to the roofs of adjacent buildings.

Clay Hopper heard his whole team jeered to the echo. He also saw them win only one game of the three, with Robinson turning in a single hit. This was the batting champion of the league, who had hit for a tremendous .357 in the league playoffs. But he did perform sensationally in the field.

Back in Montreal it was different. Maybe it was the home crowd, which had made Jackie and Rae feel most welcome all Summer. Or maybe it was just good Louisville pitching. But with record crowds cheering his every move in Canada, Jackie Robinson went wild at the plate, on the base paths and in the field. Once again he was a pace-setter, hitting with such fury and regularity that he closed the Series with a batting average of .333.

Montreal swept the three games, and became undisputed champions of the minor leagues. The French-Canadian fans went berserk in a manner never before seen in a baseball park. They spilled over the grandstand wall in a human cascade, singing the "Marseillaise" and the Canadian national anthem, and they formed a snake dance. They captured Jackie Robinson, the Negro, and Clay Hopper, the manager from Greenwood, Mississippi, hoisted both to their shoulders, and paraded around the field voicing their unconfined joy.

It was not a triumph of Negro or white. It was a triumph of baseball, for as the Virginian Cox had so astutely prophesied, success at bat and in the field will render the true baseball fan color blind. Those riotous French Canadians were not carrying men of race. They were carrying men of a national sport that captures the heart and fancy at a younger age than any other medium devised by the mind of man.

The Montreal snake dance was a signpost of the future.

The trouble ahead, anticipated by President Frank Shaughnessy, failed to materialize, and none was happier to admit it than the blustery Shaughnessy himself. His chief difficulty was handling the large crowds in all the cities of his league on Saturdays, Sundays and holidays. A new era of league prosperity had arrived.

Branch Rickey had watched every move by his Montreal team and by his Negro player. A considerable portion of the press wrote off the Robinson success, declaring that he had "played over his head." Another portion began to speculate on whether or not Jackie Robinson would be brought up to the Brooklyn Dodgers immediately, eventually, or not at all.

While speculation was rife on this last point, two dramatic incidents occurred in the office of Branch Rickey where only a year before the most dramatic of events had taken place.

President Frank Shaughnessy was an early caller, but now he wore a wide smile. Happy over his old friend's success. Happier over the prosperity of his league. Happy because of no "incidents."

Since Robinson had been signed to a Montreal contract, baseball law stated that he could be left with the Royals without fear of drafting by a major league club. He could also be brought up to Brooklyn for trial. He could be signed by Brooklyn after the purchase of his contract, and optioned down to Montreal. Which would it be, Branch?

Rickey confessed that he hadn't given it a serious thought. His own Dodgers had tied the St. Louis Cardinals, his old team, for the National League pennant, missing the World Series by an eyelash. The Brooklyn Dodgers had drawn nearly one and three-quarter million fans. Playing personnel had to be strengthened, but—.

"Of course, you do what you think is best, Branch," Shaughnessy said, his red face all smiles. "You did six months ago. But we had a record year in our league. Everybody liked Robinson, and I think he may need the steadying experience of one more year. If there is any possible way for you to leave him at Montreal, for heaven's sake do it!"

The second was a visit from Clay Hopper, his last appearance in the Brooklyn office before shoving off for Greenwood, Mississippi, where he spends his Winters buying and shipping cotton. During the season he had made no bold appraisals or predictions involving Robinson. He had not said much of his feelings, satisfied that the statistics told the story. But it is a fact that he was visibly moved many times during the year by the manner in which Robinson conducted himself on the ball field under conditions and hardships that would have broken the spirit of almost anyone else. He saw the Negro take epithets, beanballs, insults and shame, including the celebrated Syracuse black cat incident which set a new low for depravity in bench-jockeying. He saw Robinson limping from a twisted ankle and often refusing needed respite in order to help the team with whatever he had left.

Hopper's failure to volunteer an opinion on Robinson's future was a disappointment to Branch Rickey, for he counts heavily on the diversified and even conflicting opinions of his minor league managers, particularly when the moving of a player is involved. And so Rickey endeavored to draw Hopper out on the subject of the Negro player. To others in the room, studying the big minor league board containing hundreds of players' names, Rickey began to doubt aloud the fact that Robinson could make it. Oh, yes, he *did* hit, and it was quite possible that he *might* hit big league pitching. But suppose he was moved up, how did anybody know that he could make the grade competitively? And his off-field activities . . . what guarantee did the club have that Robinson wouldn't . . . well, wouldn't get out of hand in some way—?

"Mr. Rickey!" Hopper exclaimed. He rose and tossed his topcoat aside. He leaned over the desk so that he would be heard. "You don't have to worry none about that boy. He's the greatest competitor Ah ever saw, an' what's more, he's a gentleman!"

Unable to reply, Branch Rickey merely beamed.

CHAPTER 12

RATHER than test the rigidity of municipal regulations in the South, Branch Rickey arranged for the Dodgers and Montreal to train in Havana for the Spring of 1947. This period was to be preceded by a series of games between the Royals and Dodgers in Panama. The Dodger squad was to be quartered within the army base at Cristobal, with Montreal on the opposite side of the isthmus in Panama City. The Sanford mass-training idea was set up in a former Naval base at Pensacola, Fla.

To capitalize on his minor league success, Robinson set off early on an October-November barnstorming tour with a team of colored players. He was guaranteed $5,000, and wound up with less than nothing, because the promoters—Negro, at that—succeeded in swindling him out of his net profits. They were supposedly responsible Pittsburgh business people, but they paid their players with checks and when the team reached the Pacific Coast, good-natured Robinson arranged for cashing them in Los Angeles. More than $3000 worth of checks, plus a $500 bus-fixing bill, bounced, cleaning the player completely. When Branch Rickey reached Los Angeles for the Winter baseball meetings in early December of 1946, he found his prize Negro infielder playing professional basketball at $50 a game in order to have money for Christmas. And there were hospital bills for the new baby.

"I'm sorry to be such a fool, Mr. Rickey," Robinson said sheepishly. "But they cleaned me. Took just about every penny of the thirty-five hundred dollars bonus you paid me. But it's a lesson I won't forget. I'll watch my money from here on out."

Despite constant prodding through the Winter, Rickey refused to offer a hint as to whether or not Robinson would play with Brooklyn in 1947. The prodding was not always prompted by curiosity; sometimes it was a hope that he never would make the final move that would break the barrier. A Negro playing in the minor leagues was definitely not the same as in the big leagues, and so long as it hadn't happened, there was a possibility that it wouldn't.

Some of the hopefuls were close to Rickey in his official family, but they offered no open objection. They simply hoped, and Rickey let them go on hoping. Seldom did he give them fuel, except in refusing to move Robinson by front-office edict.

Once he was asked about those whose hopes were strongest. Surely he couldn't deliberately hurt them. Didn't they count in his reckoning?

"Yes, they do," he replied. "Because their objections

are based on wanting me to stay out of trouble. I can't chide them for that. But they'll take whatever comes, if or when it comes.

"Alexander Pope covers it mighty well in his 'Essay on Man,'" Rickey continued, and looked at the ceiling for the words. "They don't want the Negro in the big leagues, but when it happens," and he recited,

> " '*Vice is a monster of so frightful mien,*
> *As to be hated, needs but to be seen;*
> *Yet seen too oft, familiar with her face,*
> *We first endure, then pity, then embrace.*' "

He stared ahead thoughtfully, and sighed:

"First they'll endure Robinson, then pity him, then embrace him!"

High spot of the Winter's developments in the Robinson situation was a secret meeting in Brooklyn for the purpose of tackling step Number 5 in the over-all program. It related to "obtaining the backing and thorough understanding of the Negro race to avoid misinterpretation and abuse of its meaning."

Through the efficient cooperation of Herbert T. Miller, Executive Secretary of the Carlton Branch Y.M.C.A., more than thirty prominent Brooklyn Negroes assembled at the "Y" as guests of Rickey. Miller had sent out the invitation, reading ". . . come prepared to hear Mr. Rickey and discuss with him the things which are on his mind as well as ours, in connection with projection of what seems to be the inevitable." It was a teaser, Miller admitted, and it surely got the response. Everybody came to hear the long-awaited announcement that Robinson was being promoted to the Dodgers.

The gathering, representing a cross section of Negro responsibility, comprised five attorneys, four municipal civil service employees, three dentists, three morticians, three realtors, two physicians, a teacher, a retired teacher, an architect, a minister, a Special Sessions judge, a business secretary, a veterans' counsellor, a haberdasher, a postal employee and three Y.M.C.A. executives. Branch Rickey had insisted that his friend, Judge Lazansky, be present. He and the judge, Dr. Dodson, of the Mayor's Committee, and the author, were the only white people present. The gathering was served a hot meal, for it was February 5 and the night was bitter cold, and then Rickey was introduced to receive a thunderous ovation.

He arose and clawed nervously at the chewed end of his half-smoked cigar. A trained and effective speaker, he nevertheless began his address in seeming bewilderment. He stammered and started clumsily again. He had prepared three different speeches, each approaching the delicate problem from a different standpoint. But he couldn't think of which talk to use. Figuratively, he tore up all three and talked "off the cuff." First, he reminded them that every word spoken would have to remain off the record and not repeated outside the room. He emphasized this point and fumbled on, finally confessing that he did not know how to go about telling them what was on his mind.

"You good people who have come here on a bitterly cold night such as this," he murmured, "sort of embarrass me. I know you have come to hear something else. The pleasant smiles on your faces are not entirely due to the fine chicken dinner. Well, I'm not going to tell you what you hope to hear. Someone close to me said I didn't have the guts to tell you what I wanted to; that I didn't have the courage to give it and that you people wouldn't be able to take it.

"Well, I don't believe that. I think all of us here tonight have courage enough to give or take anything. I have a ball player . . . named Jackie Robinson. He is on the Montreal team. He may stay there. He may be brought up to Brooklyn. I don't know at this point exactly what will happen when, or if at all. But I want to say that *if* it happens, if Jackie Robinson *does* come up to the Dodgers as a major leaguer . . ."

He paused and drew in a large breath.

"The biggest threat to his success—the *one* enemy most likely to ruin that success—is the Negro people themselves!"

The gasps of shock and amazement were audible as they cut through the ominous silence. Jaws dropped. Eyes blazed in indignation. It was a sharp slap against every Negro face in the room.

"I mean it and I'll repeat it," Rickey continued, and he repeated the belief. "I say it as cruelly as I can to make you all realize and appreciate the weight of responsibility that is not only on me and my associates, but on Negroes everywhere.

"Every step of racial progress you have made has been won by suffering and often bloodshed. This step in baseball is being taken for you by a single person whose wounds you cannot see or share. But he is first a ball player, and has proved himself that. He has the ability and aptitude to succeed in the big league. History shows that you use each of your steps of progress as signal victories, as you have a right to, because you have fought for them. But you haven't fought a single lick for this victory, if it is one.

"And yet, on the day that Robinson enters the big league—*if* he does—every one of you will go out and form parades and welcoming committees. You'll strut. You'll wear badges. You'll hold Jackie Robinson Days . . . and Jackie Robinson Nights. You'll get drunk. You'll fight. You'll be arrested. You'll wine and dine the player until he is fat and futile. You'll symbolize his importance into a national comedy . . . and an ultimate tragedy—yes, tragedy!

"For let me tell you this!" Rickey thundered, and his gnarled fist smashed against the table-top. "If any individual, group, or segment of Negro society uses the advancement of Jackie Robinson in baseball as a symbol of social 'ism' or schism, a triumph of race over race, I will curse the day I ever signed him to a contract, and I will personally see that baseball is never so abused and misrepresented again!"

At this point the room broke into deafening applause, and several minutes passed before Rickey could obtain enough silence to continue. Negro tears were shed openly, and there were cries for him to continue. Finally, with silence and his point won, unequivocally, he went on with a rational discussion of possible abuses, and what must be done to prevent well-meaning individuals and groups from "spoiling Jackie's chances."

The self-policing had to come from within the Negro people themselves. It had to be voluntary, the result of recognizing great hazards. The triumph had to be one of baseball ability alone, for nothing was to be proved, except that a colored boy could play big league baseball and had a right to demonstrate the fact. All other accruals necessarily had to be byproducts, secondary benefits, always the result of; never the reason for. That, he concluded, was the object of the gathering, and the explanation of its secrecy. The problem was turned over to them, and would they please lend a hand.

At the end of a long and exciting evening, a Master Committee was formed to handle the situation. It consisted of Judge Myles A. Paige, Court of Special Sessions; Stanley M. Douglas, a federal attorney; Arthur L. Funn, a mortician; Rev. C. L. Franklin, a minister; Oliver D. Williams, attorney and YMCA official; and Herbert T. Miller, as secretary and co-ordinator.

The work and value of this group can never be evaluated nor exaggerated. It directed the formation of subcommittees through Brooklyn and Harlem with a single slogan, "Don't spoil Robinson's chances!" The message was preached from the pulpits to all religious denominations. It was spoken from the rostrum of every lodge and club. It was repeated by the bartenders in virtually every cafe or saloon frequented by Negroes. "If you're drunk, don't go to the ball game." or "Leave your liquor outside the ball park."

And further, the Master Committee formed similar committees in every big league city where Robinson would play. They discouraged as much as possible the congregation of Negroes in large groups in the ball park and on special trains. As a direct result, there were no premature Jackie Robinson Days, no splendiferous presentations at home plate, no wining or dining with special gatherings and public appearances. They made it possible for Robinson to be "let alone to play ball and nothing else." And it all came out of that historic meeting in Brooklyn on February 5, 1947.

CHAPTER 13

BROOKLYN and Montreal had already started training by the time Rickey reached Panama in mid-March, 1947, and all seemed serene. The Dodgers were well fed at the Army base, and the Negro situation on Montreal was without incident. But within two days he received word that a petition had been started—a petition to prevent Jackie Robinson from joining the Brooklyn Dodgers, even though Rickey had said nothing on the subject. It was assumed by certain regulars that the Negro was good enough to make the club.

It was not a formal document, engrossed on parchment or papyrus for the archives. It was more a word-of-mouth operation, but it had definite proponents committed to obey it and to promulgate it among the players. Just who conceived the petition has never been learned definitely, and the author never came out in the open to boast about its inception. However, it was a vehicle through which the southern boys and a few sheep-like followers expressed their displeasure at the prospect of having to mingle with a Negro on the ball field in a Dodger uniform.

One veteran player, however, revolted in a quiet, half-whimsical recalcitrance, but, in doing so, revealed the depth and scope of the movement. The revolter was Kirby Higbe, of Columbia, South Carolina, who, after his third bottle of Panama beer one evening, confided to the traveling secretary along the following lines:

"Ol' Hig just won't do it. The Ol' Man (Rickey) has been fair to Ol' Hig. So Ol' Hig ain't goin' to join any petition to keep anybody off this club. That's all."

And that was enough. Word of the movement reached Branch Rickey immediately and another half-smoked cigar was heaved into a corner to alleviate his feeling of disgust. He was quartered in the Tivoli Hotel in Cristobal, and straightway arranged to have the assorted petitioners come to his apartment one by one and as soon as possible.

Rickey's prime fear of a petition was its effect upon the morale of the players. His resolve from the start of the Robinson situation was that no phase of it would be the result of force for or against. Each move that Robinson was to make had to be a natural transition, not the result of edict, legislation or front office directive. He was to progress through skill alone, and Rickey was counting heavily upon the Negro's ability to chart his own future and particularly to influence the press and public. Most important, of course, was that the players would recognize his ability in training and demand him to help them win in 1947.

But he was now at Step Number 4 in his program of procedure: A good reaction from press and public. Knowledge of any petition, big or small, was certain to influence the itinerant press who would in turn influence the public. The effect and impact would far outweigh Robinson's true value on the ball field. The players would also be influenced by a revolt among them, and there would be no demand for the Negro as a pillar of baseball strength. Their minds would be clouded and morale would suffer, defeating Step Number 6.

Rickey decided to use some of the petitioners' tactics by enlisting the help of his "glue-man" on the team, Eddie Stanky. The Brat had acted like one at contract-signing time, and had wheedled a large chunk of cash from Rickey as a raise, but this did not lower the Dodger president's opinion of his value as a team man. Stanky was summoned to breakfast at the hotel one morning. With almost no exchange of words, Stanky intuitively seemed to know what was on the boss's mind. He understood the problem immediately.

"When you gave me that raise in February," the player said, "you told me you were doing it because you might need a favor from me some day. Well, Mr. Rickey, you've got your favor. Don't worry about a thing."

Exactly what Stanky did was not revealed, but it was apparent that he had the effect of stopping growth in the clubhouse and on the ball field. Meanwhile, Rickey prepared to tackle the recalcitrants singly and arranged for the interviews that evening. He was not worried so much about those players easily led. He was more concerned about boys from the South whose upbringing had made it impossible for them to recognize the liberty and justice of a Negro in organized baseball.

But the interviews and harangues were heated, even though the cornered petitioners had no specific defense for their actions. Just why the news of the petition failed to spread like wildfire will never be known, because his apartment was in the corner of the hotel, facing the balconies and with slatted hall doors and open French windows. Rickey outdid Stentor at his best as he hurled some of his best verbiage into the tropical night. He cut the props from one player after another with telescoped lectures on Americanism. Several of the petitioners were ashamed and gave ground. One did not. He took the worst tongue lashing of all. And when Rickey thundered at him: "Do you want to play on the same team with Robinson?" he replied, "No, suh, Ah do not!"

"Would you like your contract transferred to another club?"

With his nose almost touching Rickey's, he replied, "Yes, suh, Ah would. But Ah don't want to be made a goat of a mess Ah didn't create!"

"Then I may accommodate you, sir!" the Dodger president exclaimed. "Good night!"

And the boy left the room with flashing eyes, fists clenched.

Rickey was visibly moved by the emotional strain of this last interview. His hands trembled and he couldn't light a cigar. His voice was hoarse. It was pointed out that the player had stood up remarkably well under a heavy harangue. Rickey nodded in agreement. When reminded that the player must have been quite a soldier in the recent war, Rickey agreed.

"Yes, he must've been quite a soldier," Rickey sighed. "We were lucky to have that kind fighting for us."

It might be noted here that the unwavering petitioner was not traded in reprisal. He wasn't traded at all. He was a third-string catcher who couldn't even make the team, but he had plenty of backbone. Branch Rickey doesn't like to lose boys of that stripe, even though they fight for a lost cause. This player, he reasoned, had grandparents who fought the same way, and so came honestly by it. Some day the boy would learn that he was wrong—100% wrong.

And so he did, before the 1947 season was half over. He became a friend of Robinson's on the ball field, and proved of considerable help in Jackie's development. Moreover, he was of great help to the team and to the club in public relations during the Winter. When a managerial post opened up the following year, 1948, Rickey decided that the situation called for backbone. And so Bobby Bragan, the Carolina boy who "defied" Rickey, went to Fort Worth as manager in June, won the pennant and playoffs, and won the pennant again in 1949. In fact, he became about the best and most popular manager in the history of Fort Worth baseball and one of the Dodger organization's proudest products.

It was unfairly supposed that Dixie Walker initiated the anti-Robinson petition at Panama. No attempt by the Brooklyn club ever was made to prove or disprove this supposition. Dixie had left Panama the day before Rickey's arrival in early March. He was on his way to

Florida to meet Mrs. Walker who was indisposed at Miami. He remained there a few days, and then proceeded to Havana where the Dodgers and Montreal had reassembled to continue the training period.

But now the subject of Jackie Robinson and his immediate future was on everybody's lips and in every head. Branch Rickey had given him a first-baseman's mitt in Panama, and the Negro had taken to the bag with characteristic aptitude and skill. Moreover, he had hit the ball better than any player in either camp, batting .625. There was no doubt about him being the strongest of candidates for the Dodgers. The question was, how soon? And what was Branch Rickey doing anyway, vacillating like this? Did he think he was kidding the public or the press? Why not come right out with it and end the phony suspense?

The pressure of insistence was exactly what Rickey hoped and dared at times to anticipate. Even Clay Hopper's patience was tried. Montreal had no first baseman, while Brooklyn had two. If Robinson was headed for Brooklyn, when was Hopper to get his replacement? And who was he?

"Why don't you take Robinson to Brooklyn now, Mr. Rickey?" Hopper pleaded one evening in Havana. "He's ready. He can't prove any more on my team. Besides, I got to break in my regular first baseman pretty quick."

The tension and indecision evidently affected Jackie, because he gave indication of losing both hope and faith.

"I wouldn't say my chances look too good," he declared in Havana during March, in a workout at the Military Academy where the Royals were quartered. "They've got a mighty fine club over there. With men like they've got, I don't know if they could use me."

In addition, a bothersome callous on the underneath part of his right big toe had to be lanced. He refused to leave the lineup, and had the trainer pack the toe in cotton batting. It left him limping. Branch Rickey made him a present of a pair of new shoes, larger size. But this couldn't seem to raise Jackie's spirits. Not even the constant cheering for him by the sparse Havana crowds helped.

"I don't think they're going to do it," he confided to Bob Cooke, correspondent for the New York *Herald Tribune*, and later sports editor of that paper. "I don't think they're going to give me a chance. But it's all right with me. I'll go back to Montreal and play as hard as I can, anyway."

After that he suffered a severe stomach disorder, a type of colic, and then a siege of dysentery. He had just about everything—everything but a Dodger uniform.

Doubts were everywhere, but Branch Rickey refused to abandon his program of procedure; not even for a colored boy who was fast losing hope . . . and faith.

As this situation headed toward a climax, Dixie Walker made one of the most amazing decisions in baseball history; one that recalled his crisp comment made at the time Jackie was first signed: "As long as he isn't with the Dodgers, I'm not worried." On March 26,

1947, Dixie requested his transfer to another club in writing:

Dear Mr. Rickey:

Recently the thought has occurred to me that a change of Ball clubs would benefit both the Brooklyn Baseball Club and myself. Therefore I would like to be traded as soon as a deal can be arranged.

My association with you, the people of Brooklyn, the press and Radio has been very pleasant and one I can truthfully say I am sorry has to end. For reasons I don't care to go into I feel my decision is best for all concerned.

Very sincerely yours,
Dixie Walker.

Perhaps in some quarters such a letter would be received with rancor and invective, but Branch Rickey viewed it as a note from a player in grave emotional difficulty. Here was a veteran, 36 years old, a hero to Brooklyn fans, perhaps the most popular of all Dodgers and a great managerial possibility, and yet he was totally unprepared to recognize or accept the equality of mankind on the baseball field. He was running from the inevitable, instead of trying to solve it in his own heart. But Rickey moved quickly to relieve the veteran's embarrassment. Within three days he had received a "deal" scribbled on stationery from the Floridian Hotel, Miami:

3/29/47

Mr. Branch Rickey—

Pittsburgh agrees to accept player Walker for $40,000 cash Gionfriddo and Kalin.

Pittsburgh Baseball Club
H. Roy Hamey
Gen. Mgr.

This might have been acceptable to Rickey but for the fact that Pittsburgh continued to block the farming out of young and green players by claiming every name on the Dodger waiver list. The Pirates were trying to force Rickey to deal by tieing up the traffic of his player movements. Rickey countered by demanding Wally Westlake instead of Kalin, and, for five minutes during the discussion of the Walker deal with Pittsburgh, the name of a .247 power hitter was kicked around.

"Oh, there's no use talking, we couldn't get away with it," Hamey muttered. "Greenberg is our present power, but Kiner is our future. If he succeeded for Brooklyn, the fans would drive us out of town."

And young Kiner in a Dixie Walker deal would have done just about that, plus turning Forbes Field into a graveyard. The new Pittsburgh owners were buying big names until they could build a younger team.

But Walker was also a substantial part of Dodger power. Always an artist at the plate and batting champion in 1944, he had hit for .319 in 1946 and had driven in 116 runs. He wasn't to be "given away" simply because he couldn't adjust himself to the presence of a Negro in a Dodger uniform. The situation simmered.

CHAPTER 14

MEANWHILE the Robinson predicament approached the stage which Branch Rickey abhors—the hour of decision. He had to "fish or cut bait." He could no longer procrastinate in the final weighing of intangible values. Time, his old ally, had become a mortal enemy.

But the problem had been virtually solved by his Dodger manager, Leo Durocher, who was exasperated with his two first basemen—big and lackadaisical Howie Schultz, and the non-aggressive Ed Stevens. Durocher was positive that Robinson could surpass both, and certainly would be no worse than either. He wanted Jackie, but quickly.

The press had definitely swung to an almost unanimous insistence that the Negro be transferred from Montreal to the parent team. Many assumed that he would be in Dodger uniform on opening day and said so in print. The work of the Master Committee among the Brooklyn colored population was in effective high gear. Branch Rickey had hurdled successfully the five stages of his long-range program without a single fault. He now needed only a demand for Robinson by the Dodger players.

This demand for skill was never expressed. Whether it would have been voiced by the team cannot be said.

Before Rickey could make the final test, and arrange the dramatic switch of Robinson to the major league on a full stage before a packed audience, the roof caved in on him. Commissioner Chandler lowered the boom with a totally unexpected one-year suspension of the Brooklyn Dodger manager, and the Leo Durocher case took every headline in the nation.

Tumult and shouting . . . radios roared reaction . . . the baseball fandom of the nation screamed approval and disapproval . . . it was the most controversial topic in the history of baseball. And while it was at full-throated volume and largest type, Branch Rickey summoned Jackie Robinson from deep slumber at the McAlpin Hotel in New York on the morning of April 10, 1947, to 215 Montague Street. They used the office of Branch Rickey, Jr., adjacent to and only a few feet from the spot in Rickey senior's office that Jackie had occupied during his memorable first visit. He quickly signed the contract, and the copy, calling for a seasonal salary of $5000, the major league minimum.

A few hours later, the press box dropped its Durocher chatter and buzzed a different tune, for during the sixth inning of the Montreal-Dodger exhibition game, the following notice was tacked to the bulletin board:

The Brooklyn Dodgers today purchased the contract of Jackie Roosevelt Robinson from the Montreal Royals. He will report immediately.

Branch Rickey

It was a whisper in a whirlwind, and the Negro had entered major league baseball.

Jackie, still in a Montreal uniform, celebrated the moment by hitting into a double play. But he was all smiles as he reached the bag, for Clay Hopper, coaching at third base, was signaling over the news. The whole Montreal bench was whooping it up. The suspense was over. Branch Rickey had done it after all.

On the following morning, Jackie Robinson boarded a rudderless ship, for the Dodgers had no manager. Clyde Sukeforth, now a Brooklyn coach, was "in charge," being senior employee of the coaching staff, comprising himself, dour Ray Blades and the effervescent Jake Pitler. But there was no locker marked "Robinson."

Old Dan Comerford, who had been Brooklyn clubhouse man for forty-five years, led the puzzled Negro from the locker room to the area adjacent and pointed to a couple of hooks.

"We're a little short of lockers, Jackie," he apologized. "Just hang your things here until we get one."

This incident was built into a situation just slightly less important than the "no-room-in-the-inn" episode of nearly 2000 years ago. A few tear-jerking writers on the more sensational sports pages used it as a lurid illustration of proof that the Negro wasn't accepted by the Dodgers at all. Look, he is hanging his clothes on a hook! Why didn't Branch Rickey prepare a locker for him? The Dodger players should be ashamed, etc. etc.

One of these columns incensed a well-meaning industrialist who was deeply interested in bettering race relations. At great expense he published the column as an advertisement, and a "social service," and called upon baseball to do the right thing by the Negro.

Actually, the incident is typical of a Branch Rickey clubhouse on opening day, due to the fact that his scouting system produces an abundance of playing talent. Jackie Robinson's uniform number, 42, reflects the situation. During the regular season a big league club carries twenty-five players and three coaches, all of whom have lockers. For the first month of the season it is permitted to carry forty players.

Well, a club simply doesn't see the necessity of fifty lockers, just to accommodate rookies for a few weeks early in the season. The tear-jerking writers of a non-existent antipathy didn't bother to say that two players, both white, also were obliged to hang their clothes on hooks right next to Robinson, and that both had uniform numbers over 40.

As soon as the oversized squad was pared, Jackie Robinson moved into a vacated locker. The name, written with indelible pencil on adhesive tape, was stripped away, and his own name substituted. Most big league clubs use chalk. And every Spring in the Majors you will see the incident repeated: hopeful rookies hanging their clothes on a hook or nail outside the locker room.

Batting, fielding and pitching—*not* rabble-rousing columns or inflammatory advertisements—create the vacant lockers. And on that day when lockers are vacated for any other reason, the game of baseball will be sick or dying.

The loss of Durocher, who was a hard-driving manager, though respected by his players, deprived the uniformed Dodgers of an opportunity to crystallize the sixth and final step of Rickey's long-range program involving the Negro and baseball. They were somewhat stunned and bewildered by the sudden suspension of their kaleidoscopic manager. They succeeded in whipping the Boston Braves twice at Ebbets Field, but it was a miracle that the harassed players found their way from base to base. And Jackie Robinson got a puny hit in six tries.

Switching to the Polo Grounds, the new manager appeared. He was 63-year-old Burt Shotton, quiet, tolerant, almost the opposite of the fiery Durocher. The players greeted him with a one-sided defeat as the Giants won, 10–4. But Jackie Robinson hit safely twice, and one of the hits was his first major league home run!

Many attempts were made to portray the Dodgers as openly hostile to Jackie Robinson. They were not hostile. There was no demonstration of any kind, beyond a few handshakes. Jackie played it safe by minding his own business, learning the hit-and-run signs and paying strictest attention during the pre-game meetings.

Open hostility came, not from his own team mates,

but from short-sighted players on other National League clubs. The Philadelphia Phillies, led by their ebullient manager, Ben Chapman, turned the Ebbets Field visiting dugout into a verbal cesspool. Human dignity has rarely sunk lower than Chapman dragged it during that late-April series, for Birmingham Ben did everything but light the fiery cross.

Robinson had occasion to visit the Dodger office immediately after the ordeal with a similar tirade that had come to him through the mails. He was still upset emotionally over Chapman's cascade of abuse. Yet, when asked if he wanted an emissary to reason with Chapman, his eyes flashed, and he declared that under no circumstances would he permit anything of the kind. He had come to the Dodger office simply to turn in what might be a serious letter.

The note sounded serious. It was an expression of filth, and dire threats to the Robinson family. After inspecting it, the then Police Commissioner, Arthur W. Wallander, doubted it as a serious source of danger, because it contained a fictitious name and address. He had traced it, and concluded that a crank who was afraid to sign his name lacked the courage to carry out his threats.

But the Philadelphia feeling maintained a high temperature. Chapman continued to pop off, and defend his foul abuse of the Negro.

"Sure, we'll ride him," he was quoted as saying. "There is not a man who has come to the big leagues since baseball has been played who hasn't been ridden."

Privately he expressed the opinion that the Negro

would destroy morale and cost the Dodgers the pennant.

The situation became so alarming as to fill the Phillies' president, Bob Carpenter, with fear of "trouble ahead." Prior to the Dodgers' first visit to Shibe Park, Carpenter telephoned Branch Rickey frantically to report the awful consequences of Robinson suiting up to play in Philadelphia. Rickey was informed that the Phillies had declared their intention of refusing to play the games, if the Negro was a part of the Brooklyn team. It looked like a strike. They were out of control. It was terrible

"Great!" Rickey roared back. "That means only one thing: we will win all three games by default, and, by the way things are going, we sure can use those victories!"

All attempts to impress Rickey with this new cry of "trouble ahead" failed to elicit anything but unmitigated delight that the Dodgers would win the easiest games of the season.

Of course, Robinson appeared in Shibe Park to play and, of course, the Phillies went on the field to play against him. The Benjamin Franklin Hotel, however, won the only racial victory in Philadelphia by refusing to accept Robinson as a guest. This was a misunderstanding, for the Dodger policy from the start was that all local Jim Crow regulations, however expressed, would not be defied. Robinson was quartered in a private home, and the Dodgers later transferred their business to the Hotel Warwick in subsequent visits to the City of Brotherly Love.

But Chapman's vitriolic harangues became subject of

national discussion and indignation with the result that Commissioner Chandler cracked down on Birmingham Ben with telegraphic instructions to confine his bench-jockeying to orthodox procedure, and to keep racial issues out of the tirades. Chapman not only obeyed, but a month later stated publicly that Robinson was a major league player and that he thought the Dodgers would win the pennant because of him!

In cracking down on Chapman for his unwarranted racial abuse on the ball field, the Commissioner was carrying out a policy that was expressed privately to Branch Rickey long before Robinson had joined the Dodgers. He assured Rickey that all matters relating to Robinson would be regarded on the basis of baseball only.

The Commissioner had been maligned on the strength of the fact that he was born and raised in the Kentucky Commonwealth, and that he would place provincialism above his moral obligations as administrator of the national sport.

"I have known colored boys all my life," he declared. "We have good ones. We have bad ones. I'm sure Robinson is a good one. If he isn't, we'll soon know it, and he won't be a ball player long. If he's the good one I think he is, neither he nor Brooklyn has anything to worry about. He'll be just another ball player."

Beginning with the Chapman crack-down, the Commissioner held right to that line of objectivity. He did have occasion to warn Robinson. He had watched all aspects from the start through his own office staff and through the eyes of special investigators. But he made certain that baseball skills alone decided all issues.

The Philadelphia story had scarcely abated when the astute Stanley Woodward, then sports editor of the New York *Herald Tribune*, somehow uncovered a plan among the St. Louis Cardinals to strike on May 16 before agreeing to play a game against Jackie Robinson. This was not exactly news to Branch Rickey. He had heard no specific information, but the possibility of an early May strike had filtered through the "gripevine." He refused to take it seriously.

"You couldn't get enough ball players to agree on any one thing to pull a strike," he scoffed. "It's bogey-man stuff."

But Woodward threw a scare into everybody, particularly the National League president, Ford Frick, who immediately contacted Sam Breadon, owner of the Cardinals. Breadon flew East and went into conference. Visibly affected, he doubted that any such move would be tried, and that it seriously existed.

But Woodward had a story and flashed advance proofs to prove it. There was no alternative for President Frick, and so he laid down the law, despite Breadon's insistence that the proposed strike was not a reality.

"If you do this," Frick told the St. Louis players through their president, "you will be suspended from the League. You will find that the friends you have in the press box will not support you, that you will be outcasts.

"I do not care if half the League strike. Those who do will encounter quick retribution . . . The National League will go down the line with Robinson whatever the consequences. You will find if you go through with your intention that you have been guilty of madness."

And once again the cry of "trouble ahead" was an empty echo. The Dodgers appeared against the St. Louis Cardinals, and played the scheduled games. On the occasion of the Dodgers' first appearance in St. Louis, the Cardinals took four straight in the presence of nearly 100,000 fans. After one look at the opening-night crowd, Rickey said:

"Within a year Sam or William (Breadon and De Witt, presidents of the National and American League St. Louis teams) will have colored boys on their rosters."

Meanwhile, Rickey redoubled his efforts to accommodate the troubled Dixie Walker, who was playing every game and straining his aging legs to the utmost. Moreover, he was hitting well. The veteran flychaser was offered to the New York Giants at the opening of the season, along with left-hander Vic Lombardi and outfielder Carl Furillo in exchange for Johnny Mize. This was only the start of what might have been a big interborough deal, but it was quickly refused.

Pittsburgh's interest in Walker was finally crystallized after they had "forced" Rickey into a gigantic player-transfer in mid-May. The Pirates took five Dodgers, Kirby Higbe, Calvin McLish, Hank Behrman, Gene Mauch and Dixie Howell for little Al Gionfriddo and a sum said to be $275,000. A few weeks later Rickey sought additional pitching relief, and agreed to accept the Pirates' offer of right-handed Nick Strincevich and $40,000 for Walker's contract.

The deal was to be consummated on a warm June night at Ebbets Field in Rickey's upstairs private box where John Galbreath, part-owner of the Pirates, would see his team play the Dodgers. In a downstairs box next to the dugout was another part-owner of the Pirates, Bing Crosby, drawing almost as much attention from the overflow crowd as the ball players. This was the night Walker was to change uniforms. Rickey had made up his mind.

It was also the night during which Pete Reiser made his last crash into a concrete wall. Chasing a line drive from the bat of Ralph Kiner, the little outfielder nearly killed himself and was carried out on a stretcher with a fractured skull. Rickey could hardly spare another left-handed power hitter, and the Walker deal was reluctantly cancelled.

CHAPTER 15

BRANCH RICKEY's oft-expressed fear that public adulation, attention, invitations and correspondence would jeopardize Robinson's ball-playing was justified in the early weeks of the 1947 season. The mail was overwhelming. Jackie's modest home on McDonough Street was besieged. It was necessary to give him police protection at the ball parks against exulting fans, particularly youngsters.

Most difficult of all was the mail. Jackie was flattered and captivated by most of the letters, and insulted by some. He and his wife used every minute of spare time to read and answer the complimentary messages. Then they had to use time that couldn't be spared. Meanwhile, the Montague Street office switchboard was clogged with telephone calls for personal appearances, commercial offers, and pleas for the Negro's address or telephone number.

"It'll ruin him!" Rickey stormed. "I'll lose my ball player. He's not hitting. It's that mail. I've seen it happen before. How can you hit a curve ball while you're thinking of letters and offers and anything but the curve ball? I'll lose my ball player, that's what!"

There was no doubt that the effort of reading and trying to pen answers to the avalanche of mail was affecting Robinson's game. He suffered a severe batting slump during those early weeks, at one period going to the plate nineteen straight times without making a base hit. He was within a single day of being benched. The slump wasn't entirely due to the heavy mail and attention, but the adulation was a factor.

Rickey corrected the situation quickly by ordering that all of Robinson's mail be turned over to a special secretary for handling. He directed that all matters pertaining to Robinson be cleared through the desk of his then Assistant, the author of this book. Jackie heaved a sigh of relief and settled down to the business of base hits.

The clearance of mail and matters through special channels result in a single policy of public relations procedure, the first of which was that Robinson could accept no invitations to appear at public functions. He appeared with the team at kid-functions, but never as a special guest. Acceptance of one meant disappointment to a thousand. Through this ruling, dozens of special "honors" by well-meaning race-conscious groups were declined with thanks.

Branch Rickey's invitations to speak, always heavy, were suddenly quadrupled, and totaled 247 for the calendar year. Fifty-three of these were associated with special awards or honors for bettering race relations. The Dodger president declined virtually all of them, particularly the awards, stating that he had "brought Robinson in as a baseball player to win a pennant, and all other aspects are incidental thereto."

Robinson did make one "public" appearance, a forgivable exception. A resolve from the start was that he would avoid the threadbare publicity stunt, the "visit-to-the-kid-in-the-hospital." But the plea came from a sports writer in Connecticut through Dan Parker's New York Daily Mirror column. A Negro boy had been horribly burned on New Year's Day, 1947, in a gasoline fire, and had lain for six months in the Middletown Hospital. There was very little of him left from the waist down. His mother was working at the hospital in an effort to help pay the cost of endless skin-graftings and transfusions. She felt that the boy would never recover, if he didn't see Jackie.

And so Robinson detoured at New Haven on his way to Boston for a series. But he made the trip on two conditions: that there would be no reporters at the hospital, and that there would be no photographers.

Jackie appeared at the bedside and introduced himself. The boy blinked. Jackie offered an autographed picture of himself as proof, but the boy said nothing.

"That's funny," his mother murmured, "he's been chattering away about you like a parrot, Mr. Robinson."

"Maybe this'll loosen his tongue," Jackie said, and produced a baseball signed by the entire Dodger team.

The boy took the ball, opened his mouth, but the

words failed to emerge. He tried again without success. He turned the ball over and over in his small hands and studied the writing through eyes that were fast clouding with mist. Then he managed to look up and the tears spilled over his brown cheeks. But he never talked.

Robinson received his reward six weeks later in a letter. It was a newspaper photograph of a little colored boy on crutches, walking alone from the hospital. Underneath the picture, the message was scrawled:

Dear Jackie:

We made it.

Eddie Hamlin.

The stream of commercial offers made for the use of Robinson's name during the 1947 playing season would have netted him a small fortune. Many were out-and-out exploitation, such as the idea for the "Jackie Robinson penknife."

"What shall we say," the propositioner was asked, "when the first body is found stabbed to death with this four-inch blade?"

Many propositions were laudable and sound, but all were turned down. Moreover, every piece of mail received by Robinson was answered. In addition, each letter was signed by Robinson personally. Every request for a photograph was granted from a supply of post-card size pictures of him in Dodger uniform and bearing a facsimile signature. On a few occasions, entire school-classes had to be accommodated. "Until you send them," one harassed teacher wrote, "I simply won't get any work out of my pupils. Please hurry."

Each of the thousands of replies to letters was composed with taste and forethought and presented to Robinson for signature. Occasionally he would add a paragraph and have them re-typed, or simply write a postscript. Signing replies to some of the more caustic of the letters was difficult for him, but he realized that the very freedom which enabled him to play baseball enabled the most prejudiced to write and express his opinion.

Space necessarily limits inclusion of many letters herein, but some of the pro and con correspondence is offered for perusal.

A citizen of Jackson, Calif., must have reached for his pen during the broadcast bulletin of Robinson's signing, for he wrote to Branch Rickey on April 10th:

Just a line to let you know that a lot of boys on the west coast feel bad about the deal that Mr. Chandler handed the Brooklyn Club. On the other hand the blow that the commissioner dealt was not as severe as the one that the Brooklyn Club handed itself when it signed Jackie Robinson.

From a white resident of San Diego in the same state came militant encouragement to Jackie himself:

Just consider this note as a pat on the back for holding open the gate for other boys of your color who will come along later. I use the word color advisedly, for I believe that the color of our skins happens to be geographic. When the going gets particularly tough, read the biography of Tom Paine; that'll buck you up. Don't let the ——s get you down!

An attorney and counsellor at law in New Orleans wrote a painfully bitter harangue to Branch Rickey, and included an unequivocal prophecy of "trouble ahead":

Your decision to break big league tradition by playing a negro on the Brooklyn team is indeed deplorable. In fact, it is inconceivable that any white man would force a Negro on other white men as you have done. You have forced Robinson down their throats . . . I also seriously doubt whether Brooklyn players from other sections of the country will really accept Robinson as one of them . . . You have made a horrible mistake and I predict it wrecks your team and that will be only your deserts.

A childish scrawl from a boy in Johnson City, Tenn., offers moving contrast to the attorney's letter, except in the spelling, which was just as bad:

Dearest Jackie: How are you? I hope you are well and doing fine. I know you are surprized to be getting mail from a boy in Johnson City. The reason I am writing you is because I admire you very much and I want to be a first baseman for some great team one of these days. I want to go to the school that you went to and made good this school is U.C.L.A., I have always wanted to go there since I was a little boy . . . At present I am playing first base for the "Johnson City Eagles" . . . I am a negro boy . . . P.S. Please hope that I will make a good ball player and make the major league.

An indignant resident of Philadelphia, Pa., lost no time expressing his disapproval of the Negro in baseball when he wrote to Branch Rickey in mid-April:

You are starting something at a time when all of us should be doing something to keep our country as calm as possible. If you want to do something for the negro, why not give some educated negro *your* job . . . If you were running a rooming and boarding house would you take them in? No. Would you go out with a negro? No. Would you want your son or daughter (if you have any) to marry of negro blood? No . . . I am not a Southerner. I was born in Pittsburgh, Pa. Well, Good-Nite, Dictator, and Happy Dreams.

From Mackinaw, Illinois, came the opposite viewpoint, written to Jackie Robinson as follows with 24 signatures:

We are writing you this letter to let you know we are back of you one hundred percent. We certainly wish you all the success in the world upon your debut in the National League and your new position playing first base . . . More than for any other reason we want you to be an outstanding success so that your race will win its rightful place in the majors. We do not, under any circumstances, hold with racial differences . . . We, the patients of the Oak Knoll Tuberculosis Sanitorium, wish you the best of luck.

An outraged midshipman vented his indignation beneath the gold-embossed crest of the United States Naval Academy to Jackie:

I was very sorry to learn that you received a few letters from some bigoted people. Personally I'd like to paste them on the jaw if I had my hands on them . . . I would like to say that I am in back of you 100% and hope that you lead the league. I'm all for you and so are a hell of a lot of other people for you. If I were in your spot I'd let nothing in the world stop me from reaching the top. Good Luck!

A hasty scrawl on the stationery of a Chicago hotel carried a particularly cheering message:

I'm a Swede from Minnesota. I saw the Dodger-Cub game today. I'm proud of you. So are my wife, daughter and 2 friends of ours who attended the game today. Keep pitching and God bless you.

Brief but graphic was a note from Savannah, Georgia:

Jackie Robinson: Am just writing you to wish you leadership in batting average in Nat'l League and to make good in your connection with the majors. You have a lot to hustle for, so make good is my earnest request. Just a white man ball fan.

The president of a North Carolina insurance company wrote as follows to Jackie from the "general impression" city of Durham:

This is just a line to wish you continued success in your career. The whole nation is looking to you to take an active part in winning the World Series. MORE POWER TO YOU.

Perhaps the most difficult letter to answer came from a 20-year-old Negro girl in Akron, Ohio, along with a plea for a clandestine meeting any time he was in the general vicinity of Akron. But the policy was to answer all letters, and so Jackie read and signed his name to the following:

Ordinarily, I wouldn't even consider answering a letter like yours, but I believe you need to get straightened out on a few things. A girl as attractive and intelligent as you sound certainly should have no difficulty in finding the right man and creating a sound, honest life together in marriage. You are suffering from some kind of mental delusion that can bring you nothing but trouble and unhappiness and my advice is to get interested in some kind of work outside your daily routine in the office.

When I married Mrs. Robinson, I exchanged vows to love, honor and cherish her for the rest of my life. "Honor" means just that to me, and any sneaking, skulking escapade would destroy the very thing that enables me to hold my head up high.

Just in case you might want to write me again, I must inform you that all my mail is first opened at the Brooklyn Baseball Club offices and then forwarded to me.

Yours in reproof,
Jackie Robinson

An analysis of the first month's mail showed the writers to be overwhelmingly on Robinson's side, and, within another month, the anti-Robinson writers had disappeared. The anonymous post cards, bearing threats and disparaging remarks were not counted. Most significant was that some twenty-odd replies to vicious or obscene or threatening letters were returned by the post office stamped: "Not known here" or "No such address."

By mid-season Jackie was hitting well again and, on July Fourth, his consecutive-game hitting streak ended at 21 games, one short of the rookie record, made by Johnny Mize as a Cardinal in 1936. Barney Shotton had the team at peak speed and Brooklyn fans were talking about a pennant. Another near-record was Jackie Robinson getting hit by pitchers six times in the first six weeks of the season.

The Cleveland Indians made the Negro in baseball less of a novelty by paying the Newark Eagles $15,000 for the hard-hitting Larry Doby, who reported on June 5 as a second baseman and a poor hitter. A year later he was an outfielder and a good hitter. In 1949 his average dropped 35 points, but he had good power.

Late in August Branch Rickey purchased the contract of Dan Bankhead, a pitcher, from the Memphis Red Sox of the Negro American League. He reported at Ebbets Field on August 26 and, in his first time at bat next day, hit a home run.

Still another month later, the Dodgers were winning the 1947 National League pennant. Jackie Robinson, batting close to .300, had beaten the St. Louis Cardinals almost single-handed in a pivotal series, hitting a homer, a double and four singles in 13 trips to the plate. He had laid down almost 50 successful bunts for the season, beating out 15 and sacrificing 30. There was no doubt about him now. No trouble ahead.

Hastily-expressed views were replaced by more sober reflection. Dixie Walker appeared in Branch Rickey's office and asked if there was any possible way of retrieving the ill-fated letter of March 26. The "trouble ahead" that he had anticipated also failed to materialize and the existence of the letter bothered him. Rickey retained the note and explained the series of events which had prevented Dixie's transfer to another club.

At the end of the season, after Walker had hit .306 for the year, and played in the World Series, he was flown from Birmingham to St. Paul where Branch Rickey offered him the management of that Brooklyn farm club at an annual salary of $15,000.

"I don't know," Dixie demurred. "I think I've got at least two more years of good play left. I might get thirty thousand dollars next year and twenty the year after that. What would you do, Mr. Rickey?"

Rickey shrugged. "It's fifty thousand against thirty, Dixie," he sighed. "You know what I'd do."

"Then I think I'll try to play . . . somewheres."

"Fifteen thousand is actually more than we can afford to pay here in St. Paul," Rickey said. "But I didn't want you to leave the organization without our best offer. I think I can help you get the money you want."

Rickey then asked for waivers on Walker for purposes of unconditional release, with the claimant of his contract to pay one dollar. Inasmuch as Pittsburgh had finished last in the National League race, Pittsburgh claimed first. Walker was awarded to the Pirates. Ordinarily, that team would have paid $10,000 for his contract, but the dollar waiver price enabled them to add that sum to a salary of $20,000 and pay Walker an aggregate of $30,000 for 1948.

Rather than announce that Walker was "traded for a dollar," Rickey added Dixie's name to a later multiple-player deal with Pittsburgh. And of course, Rickey was belabored in print for cruelly "peddling" the most popular player that Brooklyn ever had.

The Brooklyn Dodgers not only turned their Borough upside down, but reversed most of the opinion regarding the Negro and baseball. One of the sharpest turn-abouts was made by the St. Louis *Sporting News*, the Bible of Baseball, which had hastily described Jackie Robinson as

". . . eligible for a trial with, let us say, the Brooklyn Dodgers' Class B farm at Newport News, if he were six years younger . . . and if he were white."

But now the high priest of baseball's Gospel, J. G. Taylor Spink, wrote a completely New Testament and flew East in time for the gigantic civic parade and celebration for the victorious Dodgers at Borough Hall. There, in a brief sermon on the mounted steps, his 20th Century beatitude informed the hysterical 200,000 fans that Jackie Robinson was Rookie of the Year!

As proof of the covenant, Spink awarded Jackie a wrist watch, which made two for him that day. The Bulova Watch Company had donated fifty wrist watches for the celebration to be distributed to players, coaches, manager and a few Dodger executives.

Almost every day for the remainder of the year brought a climax to Jackie Robinson. The loud and insistent clamor for a "day" in his honor, which had begun with his joining the Dodgers, was answered. A committee representing all the groups was permitted to hold Jackie Robinson Day at Ebbets Field on September 27, a Saturday, next to the last day of the regular season.

With the pennant cinched, a crowd of 26,123 turned out for the long-awaited day, and it seemed as though everybody brought a gift of some kind. Mallie McGriff Robinson was there, resplendent with lovely orchids and a lovlier smile of pride. For more than an hour she heard her distinguished son showered with praise and gifts.

More notable, however, was the fact that Jackie could

have finished the season with a batting average of .300 by getting three more base hits. He might have obtained these by bunting "for the average." But he never even tried.

"He was on his own," Manager Shotton said. "He could have bunted for his average, but he refused to bunt, unless the situation called for it. He hit away and took his chances of making it fairly or not at all."

The spotlight was on Robinson as the first Negro to play in a World Series, but the beam soon switched to highlight performance, and Jackie was just another ball player. He played errorless ball, drove in two runs, scored three and whacked out seven hits in 27 times at bat. The Dodgers lost after seven thrilling games, which were distinguished by the Lavagetto double to win the fourth game, Gionfriddo's catch to save the sixth and Joe Page's relief pitching to protect a slim Yankee lead to the finish of the seventh.

With the "wraps" off, Jackie began a brief barnstorming trip, and then in late October began a series of personal appearances at theaters. He was on his own, to live his life and conduct his affairs as best he could. The Brooklyn Baseball Club wanted him to be just another player, another citizen, capitalizing on opportunities which it had been necessary to deny him during the baseball season.

The high spot of his personal appearance tour came in mid-December when he was honored by the Bruin Club of UCLA in Biltmore Bowl, Los Angeles. There, with nearly 2000 looking on, Jackie Robinson returned to the scene of his humble beginnings. And he heard Los Angeles' Mayor Fletcher Bowron say:

"You, Jackie Robinson, have not only brought national credit to your alma mater, but, by your actions, have reflected outstanding credit to Los Angeles and to all members of your race. Official Los Angeles is proud to welcome home one of its most famous sons and we extend to you every best wish for your continued success."

CHAPTER 16

AFTER considerable trouble and inconvenience, the Brooklyn Dodgers and the Montreal Royals were flown to the Dominican Republic on Feb. 29, 1948 to begin thirty days of training. Though it meant transportation of more than 100 humans and a fortune in equipment, Branch Rickey was firm in his determination to patronize foreign hospitality until Negro baseball players and white baseball players could train together in any part of the United States.

And Jackie Robinson checked in carrying nearly thirty pounds more than his best playing weight!

He had picked up excess poundage fast after the World Series. He hadn't trained, or even exercised, except to reach for another portion. The long waits in dressing rooms between performances, the room-service meals at good hotels, and the rigors of the banquet circuit had made him roly-poly. While it saddened Branch Rickey, it did not surprise him.

"This proves he's just another ball player," the

Dodger president sighed. "Well, that's what I wanted."

But he was worried about more than the tragic extra weight. Robinson had been disclosing for several months an eagerness to rush the task of becoming "just another ball player." The last thing that Rickey wanted was subservience or an "Uncle Tom" attitude on the part of the Negro player, but no aspect could be changed by force.

He had spent most of the afternoon on Feb. 11 discussing salary with Jackie and Mrs. Robinson, and discussing it with considerable vehemence on either side. They were not intemperate at any point, but it most certainly was a wholehearted confession of merits and demerits in the sphere of supply and demand.

"Imagine that!" Rickey declared after it was over. "The boy was able to defend his position without fear or any other factor affecting his thinking. That's good."

But Robinson's failure to keep an important date at Newport News in early January to help launch a drive for funds to build a War Memorial Stadium was not good. Jackie had blamed Leo Durocher for a previous mix-up on the Pacific Coast. Leo, reinstated to his managing job in December, had blamed Robinson. It did not augur well for their relationship.

Rickey had spoken for fourteen hours at meetings on the Virginia peninsula, apologizing for Robinson's absence and trying to make up for his failure to appear. More than 60,000 Negroes were disappointed. The entire student body of Hampton Institute sat in stunned silence as Rickey announced that Robinson was "... unavoidably detained by a misunderstanding."

"But he'll be down here," Rickey added vehemently. "He promised the visit and he'll keep the promise!"

Through the Winter there were other instances of Jackie's eagerness to be a hail-fellow, well met, instead of a baseball curio. He was quoted constantly, which was to be expected, since he was feted regularly. He was quoted as asking a Philadelphia audience for an opinion on what he should demand for his 1948 season, and the gathering replied, "Twenty thousand!" It was good for a laugh.

On a festive occasion in Chicago he was quoted as stating that his 1947 salary was $5500, which was not a fact. His salary was $5000, and he had borrowed $500 from the club after the World Series. The loan wasn't cancelled until he had signed his 1948 contract.

Robinson's excess weight was a shock to the three coaches, Sukeforth, Blades and Pitler. On the day after the 1947 World Series they had gone far out on a limb for Jackie by stating, in Rickey's annual evaluation of all club personnel, that either Robinson or Eddie Miksis or both would take Eddie Stanky's job at second base. The majority agreed that Robinson would beat out Miksis. This made Stanky expendable for trade, if the demand for him arose.

But the coaches had evaluated Jackie on the basis of 195 pounds of lean muscle. The Robinson who reported in the Dominican Republic was an unreasonable facsimile of the whippet-like speedster that had finished the 1947 season in a blaze of baseball glory.

Durocher was not only shocked, but angry. He was on the spot to improve upon Shotton's record. He had approved the decision to trade Stanky in the Fall of 1947 by telephone from California. He had agreed that both Robinson and Miksis would beat out Stanky and that the Brat could be traded. Rickey consulted both Shotton and Durocher on this matter long before he even had an offer for Stanky, because he was not certain of his manager for 1948.

Despite the perfect climate of the Dominican Republic—sunny warm days and cool nights—Jackie Robinson discovered that his marvelous physique, now in its 30th year, would not respond to ordinary reducing measures. He had to take it slowly for fear of tearing cobwebby muscles and unused tendons.

Both Rickey and Durocher accused him of not working hard enough. Durocher declared to the press that the Negro wasn't hustling. This was a direct insult to Robinson, for he had always hustled. Durocher went even further: he charged that Robinson wasn't leveling, that he was actually loafing.

Members of the itinerant press seized on the situation as an excellent source of news. Robinson's weight and his efforts to reduce it became the big item of their dispatches. Jackie assured one and all that he had taken off twelve pounds in eleven days. This was probably a fact, but he was still another twelve or fifteen pounds from his 1947 playing weight.

Durocher took no chances. He shifted Jackie to second base to sink or swim.

"It was good enough for John McGraw and it's good enough for me," Durocher declared. "There's nothing like stooping for ground balls to reduce the waist line. What's more, Robinson will shag flies till his tongue hangs out. Jake Pitler will see to it that Jackie chases every fungo up a palm tree for the remainder of the Dodgers' stay here in Ciudad Trujillo!"

Jackie's temper was strained to the breaking point. He was plagued by writers trying to get him on a scale. Moreover, Branch Rickey sold Eddie Stanky's contract to the Boston Braves. It was Robinson or Miksis now at second base. And the extra ten or twelve pounds just wouldn't melt off. Now his arm had developed a soreness.

The excess weight continued to slow Robinson down, even during the history-making exhibition games in Texas and Oklahoma. Record crowds and overflow attendance, created chiefly by exulting Negro patrons, were surprised that the most publicized player since Babe Ruth failed to run with dazzling speed or field with reckless grace and abandon. But Jackie simply couldn't without tearing himself apart, and he had too much sense to fight a stubborn enemy the wrong way. It would take time, and it did.

Jackie Robinson wondered if his luck had run out. Most certainly his patience had. He shouldn't have read the daily papers, but he did, and one day after the start of the 1948 season he read that he had "waddled" after a ground ball. He fought against tears. No one wrote of how he had worked and was working; how he was undergoing the torture of hunger again in order to diet. His temper flamed. His weight was being blamed for the team's low state.

When the writer of the "waddling" line spoke to him in the clubhouse next day, Jackie's tongue lashed out in reprisal. The writer flashed back and declared that Jackie's use of obscenity was uncalled for. On the following day the columnist of the same paper announced to his readers that Jackie Robinson was developing a swelled head to match his mid-section.

But the excess poundage retreated before Jackie's onslaught of action. A month after the opening of the season he was gaining speed. The soreness had disappeared from his arms and legs. At Cincinnati he raced with much of his old time speed toward first base, only to see Ben Zientara, the second baseman covering first on the play, move into his path.

Jackie couldn't check his speed or even alter direction. He twisted, but not enough. He collided with the infielder with all the momentum of his 200-plus pounds in a sickening crash. Zientara flew one way and Jackie the other. The Cincinnati crowd booed the Negro as Zientara was carried off the field unconscious. Jackie was conscious but didn't dare move.

"I thought for sure this is the end," he declared later. "I couldn't feel a thing in my left leg. I was positive it was either torn off or broken into a thousand pieces."

The leg wasn't broken, but the tendons behind the

knee had been stretched. He was out for several games and returned with the area still paining a little. But he wanted mightily to stay in the lineup and help the club, which needed more than Robinson. Somehow Durocher couldn't find the winning combination and by mid-season the proud National League champions had sunk to the bottom of the standings. Tempers flared again. The players pressed and that made it worse. Robinson was beginning to hit, but his average was pitifully low. Still, plenty of Negroes came to see him.

One Sunday at the Polo Grounds it seemed as though all Harlem had turned out in his honor, only he wasn't there. He had been detained, and he arrived on the field after the team, walking alone from the clubhouse across the field to the dugout. The banner crowd roared a welcome that lasted throughout the long march. Durocher bristled furiously at the sight and the sound.

"Well, Showboat," he snarled, "you sure know when to be late."

Jackie laughed and pleaded not guilty, but the rest of the players told him that he was stupid to make such an entrance. Durocher agreed and added more.

"The next time we play here," said the fiery manager, "I'll walk out to greet you, and I'll either get some of your applause or you'll get some of my jeers!"

What Durocher didn't know was that within a week he wouldn't even be with the Dodgers. He became manager of the Giants on July 16.

Whether it was due to the departure of Durocher, the arrival of Burt Shotton to succeed him, or Jackie

Robinson's hard work, not even Jackie knows, but it is a fact that the pendulum began to swing the other way for him at that point. He began to run bases again. He began to hit as never before, and within a month the Dodgers were in first place. They didn't hold it long. In fact they played above their heads to reach that altitudinous peak. But they proved that they were not just a one-year team. Best of all, Jackie Robinson proved he could control himself, as player and man.

He has hewed to that line, and he has grown in stature ever since. The qualities that make a champion or an artist have driven him to take nothing for granted when you're at the top. Branch Rickey reminded him of it at Christmas with a present. Jackie opened the package which contained a bathroom scale. It contained no message. The scale spoke louder than any greeting.

Also, the fact that he had hit close to .350 for the latter half of the 1948 season convinced him that he could do it for a whole year. He started the 1949 season with a blaze of base hits and continued the batting conflagration until mid-August when a foot injury hampered his movements. He was leading the league in every department. Through the last six weeks his hitting fell off, but not enough to keep him from his second batting championship. He had paced the Brooklyn Dodgers to another pennant. He was tired and foot sore, but he was the batting champion and league's Most Valuable Player by declaration of the nation's Baseball Writers.

The year of 1949 found Negro players training in Florida, playing exhibition games in Texas, Oklahoma, the Carolinas and the state of Georgia, home of the Ku Klux Klan. And what did it mean?

It meant simply that Branch Rickey had found a great baseball player who happened to be a Negro, and that, as an American, he had a right to earn his living in a professional baseball game where skill and aptitude are primary factors and all other factors secondary.

As a baseball player, he is a symbol of American democracy at work. Whether he continues to be a symbol is entirely in his own hands and feet. When they play him false on the baseball field, the decision will lie in his head. He and everyone else must bear in mind that organized baseball was part of our stratified society, and that a major change therein was made without the riot and the bloodshed that attended most previous social changes. Once the element of force is employed to enhance any factor of Jackie Robinson's life, he will encounter serious difficulty, and he may wipe out the very advantages he has gained for himself and underprivileged Negroes.

This was the warning issued to the special investigator for the House of Representatives' Un-American Activities Committee when he first approached the Brooklyn Baseball Club on the subject of Jackie making an appearance before the Committee.

The decision to develop the appearance program began on May 26, 1947, at which time Communistic groups were starting a concerted move to influence Negroes in behalf of their Marxian ideology. One of their most effective claims was that Communistic pressure had forced Branch Rickey to sign a Negro baseball player. Reiteration in the centers of large Negro population was doing its work.

Exploitation continued, investigation disclosed, particularly in New York, Chicago, Pittsburgh, St. Louis, Detroit, Birmingham and New Orleans. Inasmuch as baseball was used, though falsely, as a weapon, the special investigator turned his attention to the game itself. He called Branch Rickey on December 31, 1947, and the call was routed, like many others, to me as his assistant.

After investigating the investigator, I met him on January 2, 1948 with great secrecy in a Harlem restaurant, where he introduced himself as Alvin Stokes, a Negro, with sufficient credentials from the Federal Bureau of Investigation, Congress, the Attorney General, etc., to travel anywhere.

Basically, two points were cleared:

1. If Jackie Robinson testified anywhere, it would have to be a voluntary appearance, and what he said would have to represent his true feelings.

2. There could be no political identification whatever with his appearance, nor with the Brooklyn Baseball Club's willingness to permit him, as a contract-employee, to testify as such.

With that, I agreed first to contact Jackie Robinson to see whether or not he wished to testify for anything, or even against Communism. The subject of his political leanings had never been discussed to my knowledge.

Secondly, I agreed to consult with Branch Rickey to see if he had any objections, and I was certain he had none, since his antipathy to the Communistic philosophy is greater even than his hatred of bases on balls by his pitchers.

The House Committee continued with its plan to hold hearings and receive public testimony from prominent Negroes in the large cities. If necessary, Robinson would be flown from the Dominican Republic during training, in order to make his vocal contribution to the work. Robinson had agreed to appear, and left the matter with the schedule-makers. And then the Committee Chairman was stricken ill in the Panama area and the hearings were postponed.

Investigator Stokes maintained regular contact with the Brooklyn office through me for a period of eighteen months. During this time he was particularly helpful in conferences relating to the proximity of subversive influences to Negroes in the Dodger organization. On January 1, 1949, the Chairmanship of the Un-American Activities Committee was turned over to Representative John S. Wood (Ga.).

While Stokes was quietly amassing his inter-city evidence, Paul Robeson crystallized the situation in Paris with a declaration on April 20 that Negroes in America would refuse to fight against Communistic Russia in the event of a hot war. The statement had far reaching effect, and a survey by the Committee revealed the effect as frightening.

More than 57% of the people believed Robeson to be

spokesman for the Negroes in the United States. The Committee ordered Stokes to assemble his witnesses for an effective reply to this indictment of Americanism.

The 1949 baseball season had started, and the task of coordinating a hearing with the major league schedule, or vice versa, was difficult. Jackie was alerted on the road, and seven other witnesses had to be ready. Jackie prepared to fly from either Chicago or Cincinnati and did neither. Hearings were postponed again.

Strictest secrecy had to be maintained, for the surprise element of Jackie's appearance would carry much impact. Stokes became an expert on the National League schedule and plane service to and from. It was not until shortly after July Fourth that all of his witnesses were ready. General Eisenhower, President of Columbia University, appeared and contradicted Robeson's statement with unequivocal praise of the Negroes in World War II.

It was long my belief that, regardless of what Robinson said before the Committee, he would be disparaged as a "Rickey stooge," a capitalistic puppet, the victim of a clever ghost writer, and a traitor to his race. More important to me was what Robinson, the symbol of democracy at work, believed in his heart. How did that belief stack up against what he represented to millions of Americans of all races and creeds?

That was why the announcement of his forthcoming appearance before the Committee "leaked" in Washington, D. C. Stokes handled the leak, and Jackie Robinson was taken completely by surprise at Ebbets Field on the afternoon of Friday, July 8, 1949. He knew only that the appearance was expected, but he didn't know the date. He knew that the general topic was Communism, but he didn't know a single thing about procedure or what was expected of him.

And the reporter of the press association confronted him with the fact that he was scheduled to appear on Monday, the day before the All Star Game, for which he was the nation's unanimous choice. He was told by the reporter that the Committee would ask him to reply to Paul Robeson's claim that Negroes wouldn't fight Russia.

"I'd fight any aggressor," Jackie Robinson declared. "That includes *any* aggressor, as well as the Russians. I've been treated very well, and I'll fight any one who tries to take away from me my American heritage. I want to fight for my child's right to live in this country, and for any other child's.

"All I can say is that Paul Robeson speaks only for Paul Robeson. I'm not too familiar with what he said, and I'll have to study it before I can comment further on it."

These words came from Jackie Robinson's heart as he stood on a baseball field, clothed in the uniform of our national game.

The sudden development took everyone by surprise. Later in the day the Committee granted Robinson a week's postponement of his scheduled appearance. Then, with some assistance, Jackie prepared a more formal statement, which was read to the Committee on the morning of July 18, 1949. But the meaning of his words hadn't changed.

A profoundly moved nation read his statement . . . listened to the words repeated solemnly over the radio and television . . . reiterated in magazines, editorials . . . 500,000 copies distributed to schools by Representative Arthur S. Klein, of New York . . . reprinted by the Urban League . . . solemnized in the motion picture of Robinson's life . . .

CHAPTER 17

Returning from the nation's capital by plane, Robinson suited up that night at Ebbets Field and closed the memorable July 18 in a blaze of glory. His resounding triple to the far corner of the park featured the Dodgers' victory and delighted a sell-out crowd. It also advanced him in the race for the National League batting crown.

Jackie had moved into the lead on June 9 with a .348 average, and followed with two weeks of relentless hitting that pushed the figure to .366. It seemed as though he would soar to the magic .400, but the goal eluded him when his luck ran out.

His place in the lineup was all but ended by a strained ligament in the arch-area of his right foot. He needed rest but he wouldn't ask for time off. Daily action not only increased the pain, but prevented healing. He limped badly. His field movements to right and left were shortened by a stride or two.

One New York sports writer held his own interview

and examination of the ailing foot in Philadelphia during a late-August visit and decided that Robinson couldn't play any more. Jackie also doubted that he could. The writer so informed his readers through a noon-day bulletin, announcing that the star would miss the night game and perhaps the next eight or ten. The Dodgers' chances of forging ahead of St. Louis were endangered, he added.

Jackie sat on the bench in uniform that evening, thoroughly agreeing with the itinerant scribe. He had been obliged to pass up batting practice and the fielding workout. Now he was waiting for Manager Shotton to give him the evening off; but no word came.

As the ground crew manicured the base-paths, Jackie picked up his glove with a sigh and limped into a little pitch and catch, but he remained near the dugout with his eye on Shotton in the event of "consultation." The white-haired manager didn't seem to know that Robinson was in the ball park.

"Okay," Jackie muttered to himself, "if the club needs me *that* much, I'll play on one leg."

Meanwhile, Shotton wrote the Brooklyn lineup on the card and handed it to Captain Pee Wee Reese, reasoning that Robinson in any condition was better than no Robinson at all. Besides, it was up to the player to make the first move.

And so Jackie started the ball game. In the very first inning he had the misfortune to hit a slow roller to shortstop and throw himself into a desperate race to the bag. Forgetting his foot, he thundered down the basepath, only to be thrown out by a half-step. Luckily the foot was so numb he couldn't tell whether he had a foot at all.

He played the full game that found the Dodgers trailing by two runs as they went to bat in the ninth. There, with two runners aboard, Jackie caught hold of a pitch and blasted a home run into the left field stands to give the Dodgers a badly-needed victory.

It was this game, more than any other, that made the Brooklyn players deeply conscious of Robinson's explosive value. It installed him as a psychological factor, a bellwether, a spark-plug, a take-charge player. Of course, they had known of and appreciated his great skill and even his hitting ability, but they hadn't thought of him as a "glue man" in the Stanky tradition. Now he was actually holding the team together with his consistency, dependability and his penchant for doing something important or dramatic sooner or later in each game. Branch Rickey had often described this value in speaking of the dynamic John L. "Pepper" Martin.

"If the game goes long enough," Rickey would say, "Pepper Martin will win it for you."

Robinson's emerging as a team fulcrum in August of 1949 paralleled the rise of Pee Wee Reese as field leader. Though appointed Captain before spring training, it was not until mid-summer that the little shortstop threw off a cocoon-like shyness and really acted for Manager Shotton during split-second emergencies. He assumed responsibility for defensive shifts, sign relays and the passing of information from the field, particularly about the pitcher, to the bench.

At his side, a bulwark of defensive intelligence and

quick cooperation, was Jackie Robinson, the colored boy from Pasadena; the same Negro whom Reese had befriended one dark day early in 1947 by running across the field to halt catcalls from a hostile bench merely by standing at his side. Here was a player, born and raised in a segregation state, Kentucky, coordinating with a Negro on the ball field and depending upon reciprocal coordination from the Negro in order to achieve success for the team on the playing field.

This was the Branch Rickey dream come true, and the only thing he ever tried to prove: that real baseball playing transcends all theories of class, race, religion, color and politics. The play is indeed the thing, and success on the sporting field has to spring from skill alone and the amalgamation of all skills for the good of the team!

Despite the daily pain in his foot over a period of two weeks, Jackie Robinson managed to appear in all 156 games played by the Dodgers. It was a costly display of courage in one way, because, by favoring the injury, he hit off stride. He lost his accurate touch and his batting average slumped woefully. When his hard hitting was needed most during the September drive, he was batting at a .220 pace. He was lame and tired, but he was better than "no Robinson at all."

Others on the team picked up the slack, particularly Carl Furillo, who hit well over .400 for the closing weeks. And the Dodgers, fighting in second place behind the Cardinals, literally backed in when the gasless Gas House Gang blew their lead in the final week. The

Dodgers managed to beat the Phillies in the tenth inning of the last day and the final putout sent Jackie Robinson jumping into the air with a leap of sheer joy. It was his second pennant in three years.

Moreover, he had managed to remain ahead of Enos Slaughter and take the National League batting championship with 203 safe hits in 593 times at bat for an average of .342. He also led the league in stolen bases with 37. The September slump had cost him leadership in total hits, runs scored, runs batted in and two-base hits by small margins. But his team had won the championship. Everything else was dwarfed in importance.

Robinson would just as soon forget the 1949 World Series, wherein the Dodgers received the very best of pitching in the first three games. While Newcombe, Roe and Branca were holding the Yankees to a total of two runs in 26 consecutive innings, the Dodgers could score only two runs in their own cause. Even Jackie made only three hits in sixteen times at bat for one of his worst efforts when the chips were down.

Following the wretched Series, won by the Yankees in five games, Jackie headed a barnstorming trip through cities of Southern states. The tour lasted three weeks and succeeded beyond highest expectations. Enthusiastic crowds greeted them everywhere. The average paid attendance was 5,942 per game, and a total of 148,561 spectators paid to see the 25 contests.

A high spot of the tour was reached in Columbus, Georgia, where a drop in temperature "froze" the thermometer at 40 degrees and stiffened an overflow crowd.

While the spectators shivered uncomfortably in the stands, Jackie went to the public address system and said:

"The unusually cold weather will affect us players as much as you people in the stands. Our hands will be numb and we won't be able to play our best baseball. All those who wish to do so, may have their money back and go home where it's warm."

The crowd cheered and applauded loudly and refused the offer. They remained seated throughout the game, which was well-played and ended in a 5–2 victory for Jackie's team over the Jacksonville Eagles.

The post-season tradition of naming the Most Valuable Player in each major league was inaugurated in 1911 by an automobile company, but methods of determining the winner have varied. Regardless of how he was selected, the recipient of the award gained a deserved and unique honor. Some of baseball's greatest players have been so rewarded, and Jackie Robinson received his accolade after the 1949 season.

He was named the Most Valuable Player of the National League by a committee of the nation's major league baseball writers, finishing ahead of a three-time winner, Stan Musial, of the St. Louis Cardinals. Understandably, the selection was additionally publicized because Robinson was the first Negro to be so named. But the writers were specific in declaring that the "novelty" of race had nothing to do with their selection.

One writer dissented. Still hostile to the idea of a Negro playing baseball with Caucasians, he openly declared that he would vote "only for the Most Valuable *white* player in the National League." And yet Robinson emerged the winner despite this last shred of bigotry.

Jackie Robinson closed out the 1949 season as the outstanding player in big league baseball, a far cry from the frightened and unknown rookie who signed a Montreal contract on October 23, 1945. In four brilliant years he had fought off the shackles of public doubt, fears, suspicion, hatred, bigotry and sectionalism. And his only weapons had been baseball and the implements thereof —a bat, a ball and a glove.

He was in demand for radio programs, personal appearances, salesmanship jobs, motion pictures. The press allowed as how Branch Rickey would have to dig deep into the Dodger treasury to make him one of the highest-paid players in the game, commensurate with his true value.

Jackie launched into a commercialization program calculated to make him financially independent, and to protect the future of his son and the daughter soon to be born. He placed his affairs in the hands of a capable attorney. He signed to do a national network radio program once a week for the year. He signed to appear in a motion picture, dramatizing the story of his life. He signed to sell commodities in a store at a weekly stipend. He arranged for the sale of odds and ends carrying his signature or his likeness on a royalty basis. He made commercial appearances on television programs.

And he devoted fifteen hours a week, without any compensation at all, to the youth program at the Harlem

Y.M.C.A. For he still harbored a hope of improving the lot of those kids less fortunate than he. His own road had been hard. He could easily imagine the difficulties facing those who hadn't been endowed with his speed and skills; who would never meet up with a Branch Rickey.

Exactly how much money Robinson made through the Winter of 1949–50 and the season of 1950, only his tax consultant knows. Most assuredly it was not as high as people imagine. Real-life sums never are. His baseball salary was announced as $35,000. It may have been more. The income derived from his motion picture deal was variously estimated at from $100,000 to a quarter of a million. Actually his deal was a cash payment of $50,-000 from which he had to pay an author $20,000. He was awarded 15% of the picture's profits, but, since the film cost about $400,000 to make, a year or two could pass before Robinson received any profits, but that was no hardship, because of the income tax situation.

More important than the money; more important than the fact that he ran into hard luck and injury again during 1950 and missed the batting championship that looked to be a cinch; more important than the loss of the pennant on the final day of the season was his "loss" of Branch Rickey.

In order to secure his own financial future, Rickey was obliged to sell his 25% ownership of the Brooklyn Dodgers at the close of the 1950 season. This meant moving to new baseball scenes, leaving all of his Brooklyn achievements to history.

It also meant leaving Jackie Robinson behind, as an individual, along with other dark-skinned individuals—Don Newcombe, Roy Campanella, Dan Bankhead. All Negroes, all individuals, but all, fortunately, great ball players, independent of sponsorship or nepotism for baseball success.

And that was the way Rickey had planned it from the start: the evaluation of Negroes on the basis of skill and aptitude. All had it, and most of all, Jackie Robinson.

Robinson felt a stab of regret when, during the winter, Branch Rickey announced his acceptance of a five-year contract as general manager of the Pittsburgh Pirates. His thanks to Rickey's foresight and courage and fairness could never be adequately expressed. But as a natural-born competitor, he had only one comment:

"I'll play my head off to beat Mr. Rickey's Pittsburgh team, along with the six other clubs in our league."

And that's exactly the way the true fan wants it: healthy competition above all other considerations, winning the games through skill, aggressiveness and aptitude.

Strange as it seemed, especially to the two principals, it was now Jackie Robinson versus his benefactor, Branch Rickey, on the ball field.

CHAPTER 18

THE SHIFT of corporate control for 1951 brought a change in Brooklyn Dodger management that cut Jackie Robinson "loose" for the first time as a player. Barney Shotton never knowingly restrained Jackie; the manager's quiet reserve was responsible. The elder-statesman quality about Rickey's white-haired friend made any player think twice before acting impulsively. For instance:

Late in the 1949 season, Robinson got the bunt sign in a game against Cincinnati in Brooklyn. "Peanuts" Lowery, playing third base for the Reds, either caught or guessed the sign. He began creeping in on the grass as the pitcher stretched and checked the runners. Soon he was "on top" of the plate, ready to smother the bunt. Jackie squared away as ordered. Then, in a split second, he swung at the pitch with all his might, hoping to slam the ball past Lowery for a base hit, or down the little fellow's throat. It was a bullet drive, but Lowery dived and speared it with his gloved hand.

"It was a lucky catch for him," Jackie sighed in recollection, "but lucky for me he didn't make a double play or worse. I crawled back to the bench with my head hanging. I peeked at Shotton, but he ignored me. So did the players.

"Shotton didn't say a word then, or after the game. I worried. No mention the next day either, or the next. Maybe I was forgiven. Even so, I had plagued myself with worry and I vowed never to disobey another sign. I was dressing for a game in front of my locker a few days later when a soft voice whispered behind me,

" 'Robinson, do you know you're fifty dollars poorer than you think you are?'

"It was Shotton. Just by keeping quiet and letting me stew in my own worry, he had punished me far more than he could have by chewing me out in the clubhouse."

Charlie Dressen, brought in from the Pacific Coast League to replace Shotton, had a different approach. It was direct, and sometimes on the spot. Charlie talked a lot on the field, in the clubhouse and to the press. He ran his team with a firm hand but gave them a sense of freedom in mouth and movement. He was completely lacking in elder-statesman quality, and, sometimes, in diplomacy.

"But without considering personalities—just management and method from a player's point of view," Jackie once said, "Shotton was not my idea of what a manager should be. He never wore a baseball uniform in Brooklyn, and he never went out on the field to argue with an umpire or talk to a pitcher. You'd be surprised at what this means in a tight ball game."

The difference in managers may seem small, but Jackie's new feeling of freedom was big. Gone was paternal Barney Shotton under whom he had begun his pioneering big-league career. The replacement was a cocky, swaggering, talkative little guy who knew the game backwards and forwards and wasn't afraid to play it either way, if it offered a chance to win. He wanted—demanded—an aggressive team. A new era had begun for Jackie Robinson. He could now "fight back," and he did. His feud with Leo Durocher had a constantly burning fuse.

He began putting together what may stand as his greatest season. He played a full schedule at second base and led the team, actually spark-plugged it, offensively from the start to the final moments of the tragic finish.

Selected for the third straight year as the National League All Star second baseman, his two singles at Detroit in July helped humble the American Leaguers, 8–3.

By mid-August the Dodgers had "sewed up" the pennant with a lead of 13½ games, only to see an inspired team of New York Giants begin a six-week drive that has no parallel in baseball history. It is not true that the Dodgers "blew up," and no one is more certain than Robinson. Injuries and poor play, yes, but no choking up.

"The suggestion is unfair to both ball clubs," Jackie insisted. "We played right down to where any kind of break one way or the other could decide it, and a single pitch did, with one out in the last inning of the third playoff game. You can't make a pennant race any tighter."

Jackie's freedom of foot and bat and tongue in spearheading the Dodgers through 1951 soon made him a target of criticism. He was, some said, "getting out of hand." True, if you compare it with the enforced you-can't-fight-back behavior of 1947. More properly, he was proving the wisdom of an old saying, "A real success made by the qualities of the thing itself is always a declaration of war." He was in the thick of the race for the batting championship and the base-stealing honors. He resented the continued brush-off pitches, nine of which struck him. He began a running feud with Sal Maglie of the Giants. "Get" Robinson, and you weaken the Dodgers.

When Brooklyn lost the vital series in Boston, where tempers of players and umpires were short, an angry Dodger kicked a hole in the door of the umpires' dressing room. A Boston reporter told the world it was "tempestuous" Robinson. Jackie failed to deny it publicly, for doing so would have meant revealing the owner of the kicking toe. And so a nation was confident of Robinson's increasing "bad behavior." When the actual kicker later disclosed his identity, the reporter quickly apologized.

"I'm sorry, Jackie," the writer said. "I recognized your voice popping off in there and assumed you had kicked the door. I was right on my deadline and didn't have time to check."

But there was no way the reporter could call back the editions and erase the headlines of false witness in screaming black type.

Final game of the schedule found the Dodgers in a situation that had been unthinkable two months, or even two weeks, before. The Giants had won in Boston, their tenth straight. The Dodgers, trailing in Philadelphia, by 6–1, needed a victory to *tie*. But they fought back, as did the Phillies, and reached the ninth inning in an 8–8 deadlock.

The Phils loaded the bases with two out in the 12th. Eddie Waitkus pulled a drive, but not enough for clean fielding. It seemed like a sure game-ender, to the right of second base. But Jackie dived, speared it a few inches from the ground, jammed his elbow into his stomach and went unconscious just as an agonizing pain knifed into his right shoulder. When he came to, the inning was over and Pee Wee Reese was kidding him about "showboating on an easy play." It was Pee Wee who prodded him into remaining in the game with the shoulder pain. Good thing he did, too, because Jackie lashed a fast ball into the left field stands in the 14th inning to win the game and send the Dodgers into the three-game playoff. It was their second pennant-tie in five years.

Jackie was a tower of batting strength in the post-season games. After the Dodgers had dropped the first at Ebbets Field, to the Giants, 3–1, his bat was responsible for Brooklyn's first three runs in the second game with a first-inning homer, a third-inning single and a fifth inning single. Clem Labine pitched a 10–0 shutout.

Moving to the Polo Grounds for the third game,

Jackie's single drove in Reese for the Dodgers' first run. In the eighth, he scored the third and last Dodger run that seemed to put the pennant on ice, 3–1. The ninth inning, of course, brought the collapse of Don Newcombe, and relief by Ralph Branca, whose second pitch was blasted into the left field stands for the most dramatic home run of all time. And while other players screamed and jumped, or moaned and slumped, Jackie Robinson followed Bobby Thomson around the base paths, making sure he touched every base.

Jackie then confounded the Giants with a surprising gesture of good sportsmanship. Though hating nothing worse than defeat, he was the first of his team to reach the Giants' dressing room with congratulations for a well-earned victory. Somehow Leo Durocher had no heart for a feud with Jackie after that visit, though he "rode" him hard during ball games.

The pennant went to the Giants, yes, but Robinson was still a hero. His batting average, .338 for 153 games, was bettered only by Stan Musial and Richie Ashburn. Roy Campanella, plagued in late season by body bruises and a bean-ball injury, was the Dodgers' only other .300 hitter, with an average of .325.

Jackie Robinson went into the record books for the best fielding job ever turned in by a second baseman. He committed only seven errors, fewest ever made in a 150-game season. He handled 825 fielding chances for an average of .992. His 137 double plays were a league record. But when this remarkable showing was called to his attention, he answered almost angrily,

"So what? We didn't win, did we?"

What Robinson meant was borne out the next year, 1952, when he turned in a record that looks disappointing on paper when compared with the season before. His batting average dropped 30 points, but his built-in scowl was almost erased by a pennant victory over the despised Giants that still has the "experts" guessing.

"The tale of 1952 is so tied up with the drama of the year before," wrote Tommy Holmes, veteran Brooklyn baseball writer in his breezy history, *Dodger Daze and Knights*, "that it has no separate entity. It is a grim tale of rehabilitation, a determined season-long drive of the Brooklyn athletes, not only to relieve the fans of that feeling of being kicked around, but to restore their own self-respect. In many respects, the Dodger victory was as amazing as their defeat had been the year before.

"No other club ever won a pennant with only one 10-complete game pitcher, and Carl Erskine hit ten right on the nose, one of which was a no-hitter against the Cubs. No other club ever won a pennant with only one pitcher who could win 15 games. But individual ball games were completely subordinate in the over-all picture to the goal the Dodgers were determined to win. This was a pennant they *had* to win. This was a must."

Though Jackie Robinson batted only .308, it was good enough to lead his team again, and five points better than the only other Dodger, Duke Snider, to top the .300 mark. His first-inning homer in the abbreviated All-Star Game was the winning margin.

But it was also one of his roughest years. The cry of "bean ball!" rose in many games. The Dodgers accused the Giants, and the Giants called the Dodgers cry babies. Whether deliberately or not, Robinson was knocked down repeatedly. He failed to escape the close pitch 14 times, for his all-time high in a single season of being hit by pitchers. The many body bruises, though, meant wildness.

"But look at my base-on-balls total for the year," he grinned.

They totaled 106, 20 more than ever before. The value of this brush-off pitching was reflected in his runs-scored. In 1951 he scored 106 runs on 185 base hits, and in 1952 he crossed the plate 104 times on only 157 hits. Bases on balls and hit-by-pitcher made the difference. On the bases he was his old sugar-footed self with 24 steals, and his home run total, 19, equaled his all-time high.

The high spot of one more World Series struggle with the Yankees came in the seventh inning of the seventh game. The Dodgers trailed, 4–2, but they had filled the bases on Vic Raschi with one out. Lefthanded Bob Kuzava relieved to pitch to lefthanded Duke Snider, who had hit four home runs in the Series. He was retired on a short fly to third. Two out. What Jackie would have given for one of his game-winning home runs at that moment! It was the spot for a base-clearing double, or better.

But Kuzava never was more effective. Jackie swung a bit under an outside delivery, lifting the ball high toward the right side of the infield for what looked like an ordinary out. A sharp wind from right field took over, blowing the ball back toward the plate. With four Dodgers racing, the Yankee infield did nothing about the towering wind-blown ball. Ebbets Field rang with frantic cries to speeding Furillo, Cox, Reese and Robinson, until second baseman Billy Martin finally charged in at the last instant, and made a diving catch halfway to the plate. It ended the rally and the inning and virtually the Series. There was no more scoring and the Yankees won again, four games to three.

James "Junior" Gilliam, a fast, sure-handed, switch-hitting infielder, became the first player to cloud Jackie Robinson's future as a big leaguer. A Tennessee-born colored boy, Gilliam reached Vero Beach in the spring of 1953 by way of two impressive years at Jackie's alma mater, Montreal. Much was made of the fact that Gilliam, not on the Dodger player-roster, had crowded past two infielding Dons who were, Hoak and Zimmer. This was because players with several years of minor league service are often promoted to the roster of the parent club in the fall to protect them from the baseball draft. With only two years in the Brooklyn farm organization, Gilliam wasn't draftable.

But he played like a veteran of many campaigns, and Robinson, whose job was in jeopardy, was first and highest in praise of the rookie. When it looked as though Gilliam had the job, Jackie moved over to third base and a rumor of "player revolt" followed. Now the popular Billy Cox's job was in danger. Some players resented this invasion of imagined territorial rights. Robinson became the center of one more storm. Questioned about it, he said:

"If the players are protesting because Cox may lose

his regular job, I'm all for them. Nobody can play third base as well as Billy. But if they're steamed because Gilliam is colored, I'm against them. I made this team by playing. Junior should have the same chance, no matter whose job is at stake."

Ironically, the foment subsided when Jackie stumbled on the porch of the off-base cottage where he lived with his family. He re-injured a weak knee and hobbled through enough of the training period to permit establishment of Gilliam as a sure thing at second base. When his knee could take heavy practice, Jackie announced his willingness to try for any job.

"I'll play anywhere Manager Dressen thinks I can do the team some good," he declared. "And I mean *anywhere!*"

Jackie Robinson became a utility player, but his solid hitting soon brought him the third-base job regularly, despite Billy Cox's best season at the plate. Fortunately it was one of the greatest of all Brooklyn Dodger teams. The lineup was packed with power. Six of them made the All-Star team: Furillo, who wound up as National League batting champion; Campanella, who became the League's Most Valuable Player and leader in runs-batted-in; Duke Snider, who led the League in run-scoring and power; Robinson at third base with a final batting average of .329; Reese at shortstop; Hodges, hitting .300 for the first time; and Erskine, who was to win 20 games, as the pitcher. The National League won an easy 5–1 victory in Cincinnati.

The Dodgers coasted to victory, 13 games ahead of the

Milwaukee Braves, who had moved from Boston during Spring training, and totaling 105 games won. Jackie had played in 136 games, and his Dodgers of 1953 finally seemed ready to beat the Yankees in a World Series. But it wasn't to be. Their power was either spotty or not at all when needed, and the pitching was unreliable. Seven of the nine Dodger regulars made 45 hits in 141 official times at bat in the Series for a combined average of .320. Even rookie Gilliam hit over .300.

The Yankees' pitching was invincible in the clutch. They took the first two games at the Stadium. The Dodgers squared it with two victories at Ebbets Field, then watched their pitching collapse in the fifth game. After Furillo's ninth-inning homer at the Stadium had tied the score in the ninth inning of the sixth game, the Yankees opened their half with a base on balls off Clem Labine, got a scratch hit to third, and Billy Martin's timely single ended the Series. Jackie played left field without an error and batted .320.

An eventful off-season period began for Jackie with a barnstorming tour, but it was climaxed by news of Charlie Dressen's surprising dismissal as manager of the Dodgers. The unprecedented move—release of a manager who had won a pair of consecutive pennants—was shrouded in mystery, suggestion of intrigue, a secret ultimatum letter by Dressen's wife, and behind-the-scenes skulduggery. Actually, there was no mystery, and certainly no scandal.

Walter O'Malley, president of the Brooklyn operation, simply agreed to return to the Branch Rickey system of selecting managers for the parent club from the minor-league organization. Under this method, the big-league manager is really an extension of front-office farm-club operation, but without loss of dignity or authority among his big-league players. He is familiar with many of his players as minor-league rookies, but, more important, he understands the front-office problems of options—the return of half-developed players to minor-league teams subject to a certain number of recalls. He builds the parent team by coordinating with the front office, especially in connection with borderline ability—keeping the player whose options have expired and sending back the player who is still optionable.

Contrasting this is the individualistic manager, the John J. McGraw type of field leader. He is not an obstructionist, but he is constantly thinking only of this year, or looking out for his own big-league reputation, sometimes at the expense of front-office operation. This is the old-school type. Dressen was and still is of this school. So are several others, though the trend in the past few seasons has been to the less colorful, organization type of manager exemplified by men such as Stan Hack, Mayo Smith, Birdie Tebbetts, Pinky Higgins, Bill Rigney and Ralph Houk. They and others who followed, were part of a new wave in managers, men who are guided much more closely by front-office thinking.

Branch Rickey was succeeded as general manager in 1951 by two excellent front-office workmen he had trained, Emil J. "Buzzie" Bavasi and Fresco Thompson. They recognized Brooklyn's need of a field manager who would foster and protect their long-range building plans. They prevailed upon President O'Malley to go along with them, though it took 18 months and though it risked good public relations, since Dressen was deservedly popular with the press. He couldn't simply be fired after two pennants.

Flushed with success, Dressen actually eliminated himself. Having beaten both Eddie Stanky and Leo Durocher, both of whom had been given long-term contracts by their club owners in mid-1953, Charlie felt that he had earned the security that a three-year contract would bring. Meanwhile, his bosses said nothing about the future, confident that Charlie would talk first. And he did.

The demand was outlined in a letter written by Mrs. Dressen. Except for a paragraph relating to a liberal and unrealistic cash allowance to be written off as "corporate expenses," the letter was wholly innocuous. It reflected only a loyal wife's justifiable concern for her hardworking and capable husband. Charlie wanted a three-year contract at $40,000 per year, with the aforementioned expense allowance. There was only one meeting.

Walter O'Malley offered a single year at a substantial raise. Dressen refused, of course, and left the Dodger office thinking there would be another meeting. He might have settled for two years. He failed to realize that his best security lay in managing under any terms for the most successful baseball organization in National League history. The World Series money was a big item. He would always have a team at the top with the Dodgers, regardless of contract tenure. Winning in the big leagues on a one-year contract is far safer than an iron-clad, long-term agreement with a last-place club.

There never was another meeting. Dressen's job was suggested—not actually offered—to Pee Wee Reese, who said that, if it were offered, he wouldn't take it. The path was thus cleared to bring up Walter Alston, manager of Montreal. It came as no surprise to members of the Dodgers organization. Alston had managed the Dodgers' Class B team at Nashua, New Hampshire, in 1946. Bavasi was business manager there at the time. Moreover, Alston had handled baseball's pioneering "colored battery," Roy Campanella and Don Newcombe, in their first year of organized baseball, 1946. Now Newcombe, an unpredictable quantity of pitching greatness and emotional unsteadiness, was returning to the Dodgers from military service.

Jackie Robinson also entered the high brackets of income. His salary as a player had reached a peak $37,500. His World Series share was more than $6000. Substantial outside income, supervised by his attorney and advisor, Martin Stone, came from personal appearances, radio and television, indorsements, and as staff consultant on youth policies for National Broadcasting Company. He also contributed free time to youth centers in New York City.

Now his family numbered three children—Jackie, Jr., nearly six; Sharon, nearly four; and infant David. After five years in St. Albans, Long Island, he wanted to move them and Rachel to the wooded hills of Westchester County, New York, or adjacent Connecticut. He sought land in several places, and met gentle but firm resistance. Eventually he had a firm deal in Westchester. Midway in negotiations the price increased by $5000, and then the deal evaporated.

A newspaper in Bridgeport, Connecticut, ran a story saying that Jackie and his family were victims of racial discrimination.

"This wasn't true," Jackie explained. "There was no open hostility. And we weren't trying to break down anything. No Negro wants to move his growing family into a nice woodsy section where there are no other Negro children. But where is there such a place *with* Negro children? You have to start somewhere, if you've worked hard, saved your money and want fresh air and country for your kids.

"But when the story appeared in Bridgeport, the North Stamford people became indignant. Ministers and prominent business people spoke up. Finally we got a nice piece of land. Rachel brought out the building plans she had saved, and the dream home was started."

Jackie gave it everything he had in spring training for the new manager, quiet-spoken Walter Alston. He finished the exhibition games with 16 hits in 26 trips to the plate for an average of .600. And the ex-infielder had beaten out specialists for the leftfielding job—George Shuba, Don Thompson, Sandy Amoros, Dick Williams, Walt Moryn, Gino Cimoli, Bill Antonello and lesser candidates.

He opened the 1954 season swinging the hottest bat of his career. He had a 4-for-4 night in the first game of a series in Philadelphia, scoring two runs and batting in three with two singles, a double and a seventh-inning homer that broke a tie. He had 3-for-2 the next night, and was horse-collared in the third game. He was also a target for Philadelphia pitchers who nicked him twice, bringing his total of hits by pitches to 61 since joining the Dodgers.

"If they keep throwing at me," he declared to Earl Torgenson at first base, "I'm going to get someone. You'd think they'd know by now that it doesn't do any good to throw at me."

He hung up another 10-for-6 streak in a three-game series at Ebbets Field in mid-May, and a 9-for-8 record in two games at Chicago in early June. By now he was streaking along with a batting average of .380. He spark-plugged the Dodgers as never before. He batted clean-up position, and delivered in spite of a badly bruised heel that forced Manager Alston to spell him occasionally. By mid-season his outfielding average was 1.000, and moved the veteran correspondent of the New York *Times*, Roscoe McGowen, to write:

"There have been criticisms of Robinson's abilities as an outfielder, including some self-criticism by Jackie himself, but the fact remains that the Dodger management has been unable to produce a leftfielder who could displace Jack. Even on one good leg, he is still pacing the team."

What promised to be his greatest year, however, soon became a nightmare. Pressures began early in the season when Roy Campanella underwent a delicate operation on his hand. The second-division Giants of 1953 were "up" again. So were the Milwaukee Braves. The competitive load sharpened Jackie's impatience, and then came one of those "breaks" that defy explanation. It boomeranged cruelly.

Playing in Milwaukee on the night of June 2nd, the Dodgers were losing in the rain. Robinson was seething, for the game never should have been started. Then, for the first time and perhaps the last, a big-league umpire gave a batter a base on balls when the count was only 3 and 2. The Dodgers stormed the umpire, Lee Ballanfant, who refused to call Johnny Logan back from first.

When he batted a few minutes later, Jackie said, "That's the worst call I've ever seen in baseball. You gave Logan first on a three-and-two count."

"Hit or I'll put you out of the game," Ballanfant replied.

"You've really messed up this game, Lee."

"You're out of the game!"

More words, and then Jackie left in a blue rage. He tossed the bat toward the tray in front of the Dodger dugout. The rainsoaked wood slid through his moist hand. He tightened the grip instinctively and then let the bat slip out. The bat soared over the dugout and into the box seat area. It caromed off Henry Yelvington, an usher. It struck Mrs. Peter Wolinsky above the left eye, and her husband on the shoulder.

Jackie rushed over, terrified and apologetic. The frightened spectators were gracious. Jackie lingered, anxiously. It was a terrible thing. He said so, and abused himself for the carelessness. The Dodgers won the five-inning game, but the bat-throwing incident made lurid headlines across the nation. Here was proof positive, readers were told, that Robinson had finally got "out of hand." His explanation to league president Warren Giles was satisfactory enough to excuse the incident as an accident. But he was fined $50 for resuming an argument with Ballanfant at the plate.

The All-Star Game, Jackie's sixth, was a free-hitting shambles, won by the American Leaguers in the eighth inning after the Nationals had "won" it in their half. It was soon forgotten in the excitement of the three-team pennant race in the older league. Writers found new ways to say that Jackie's days as a Dodger were numbered. The "retirement" stories reached a peak in late August when the Dodgers trailed the Giants by nearly five games. One die-hard Cincinnati writer was positive he was "finally seeing the last of Robinson."

"I definitely intend to keep on playing," Jackie insisted once more. "I realize my indebtedness to the game. It's been good to me and I want to keep on playing as long as I can. However, if I find I can't do justice to myself and give the ball club its due, then I'll retire."

Within a month the situation was intensified. Jackie was fined $75 and Pee Wee Reese $50 for complications arising from a dispute with Umpire Donatelli, again in Milwaukee, over a vital decision on Reese at first base. The shortstop had blown his temper. Jackie added his own fuel, and later wrapped a towel around his neck as he sat on the bench to imply that the umpire was "choking up" before a home-town crowd. The ball club had tried to keep the fines a secret, and the leak brought angry comment from the front office.

Loss of the Labor Day double-header to the last-place Pittsburgh Pirates just about finished the Dodgers psychologically. Roy Campanella, still handicapped, was batting only .207. Jackie's once-high average had simmered down to a few points over .300. He had played two infield positions and left field, batted 100 times fewer than the year before. Everything went wrong. He was even tricked out of the Dodger lineup at Ebbets Field on September 9 by a cruel and anonymous phone call saying that his baby, David, was sick and to hurry home. He left in the second inning, made a frantic call to his home and learned that it was a cruel hoax. But he was out of the game.

That Robinson was finally "through" at last, was a popular assumption, best reflected by columnist Joe Williams, of the New York *World Telegram and Sun.* He wrote that Walter Alston would be rehired for 1955, despite loss of the pennant, but that Jackie Robinson would not be back with the team.

"If my informant is correct," he continued, "Robinson's loss in popularity in Flatbush has been as conspicuous as his loss in proficiency. Robinson has repeatedly threatened to quit baseball if traded. 'Nevertheless, hot or cold, he goes this time,' says my informant. The inference was also rather plain that Jackie Boy had gotten himself an upper berth in the Bums' doghouse."

Said President Walter O'Malley, "We will not confirm

nor deny the story, but decisions on subjects of this nature are not being made at this time."

"I don't know where I'll play," Jackie sighed when questioned after the Dodgers had limped home in second place behind the despised Giants. "I hope it's here, but if it isn't here, I'll be playing somewhere."

"Anywhere?"

"No, not anywhere. That's definite."

CHAPTER 19

Jackie Robinson's tenth year in organized baseball began on notes of challenge and controversy that reverberated in varying degrees throughout 1955. It seemed strange that one who had come a long way and gained much should be so far from peace with himself and others. He was reasonably secure financially. His family was finally established in a 14-room suburban paradise with a separate room for his many trophies and citations. Jackie, Jr., and Sharon attended the local school without incident. He had won lasting renown, dignity and national respect. President Eisenhower had once crossed a crowded ballroom in Washington to shake his hand.

But he could not cloak his intense desire to continue playing baseball and winning games, nor the fear that he wouldn't be able to. It influenced his every word in public. Sometimes he sounded like the brassiest rookie, like a puppy barking to scare others while lessening his own fright.

Jackie wasn't frightened, of course, but he was uncomfortably aware of a formidable foe in his path—athletic decline. It was symbolized by his nearly-white hair, his forthcoming thirty-sixth birthday on January 31st, and, more realistically, by a forthcoming cut in salary. It would be his first since joining the Brooklyn organization, and a significant milestone. He referred to it openly, sometimes in a thinly-disguised threat to the Dodger front office. Frequently interviewed in public appearances, he was quoted and misquoted, but he was never ignored, especially in critical headlines.

As the personification of success in inter-racial amity, he made a cross-country speaking tour for the National Conference of Christians and Jews that led up to major participation in Brotherhood Week. He was now a big man, and often opinionated, but still humble enough to make a surprise appearance and talk at a Fathers and Sons Breakfast at Temple Emeth, Boston, in early January to square an old debt. A Temple member, former Boston Councilor Israel Muchnick, had befriended him ten years before when he "tried out" for the Red Sox at Fenway Park. To the reporters' inevitable inquiry after his talk, he said:

"I don't care where I play—whether it's infield or outfield. But I don't want to sit on the bench. If I can't play regularly, I'll retire and go into business."

This was not an idle threat. Careful investments had given him several business interests. Jackie Robinson Clothes, Inc., on West 125th Street, center of New York City's Harlem district, was flourishing. Flattering offers were awaiting the day when he was no longer in baseball. But less than a week after the Boston "ultimatum," he signed for a modest cut in salary, far from the maximum 25% permitted by baseball rules.

After dieting several weeks to control his weight, he opened the battle to become a Dodger regular at some position. His spirited play moved one Brooklyn correspondent to write that Jackie might go on, like Tennyson's Brook, forever. This tribute followed a 4-for-4 performance in Tampa against the White Sox. Two weeks later he appeared to have beaten all competition for the third-base job. (Billy Cox had been traded to the Baltimore Orioles.) His exhibition-game batting average was .349, and he had frequently flashed his old tantalizing skill on the base paths. An occasional bruise and arm-weariness failed to still his open claim to the regular job.

When Manager Alston failed to start him in New Orleans, Jackie voiced his angry impatience to a reporter, and the dramatic protest made fiery headlines. The "open breach" became "too wide for healing" when Jackie popped off two days later while chafing on the bench in Chattanooga. Writers wrote that this would surely tear the team asunder. Back in Brooklyn President Walter O'Malley thought otherwise.

"I'm glad to see my manager blow his top," he said. "He needs to blow it once. That's okay with me. It's a healthy sign. I'm also pleased that one of my veteran players is so keen to get in there and play that he blows his top when he's left on the bench. It's good for everybody to let off some steam."

When the 1955 season opened, Alston was pictured

with his arm around Robinson, whom he named the Dodgers' starting third baseman. Straightway from opening game Brooklyn began a winning streak that set a record before it ended at ten straight. After losing two of three near-riotous games to the Giants at Ebbets Field, the Dodgers steam-rolled again. Three weeks of play found them with 18 victories against only two defeats for a runaway percentage of .900.

This was largely the story of the Brooklyn Dodgers throughout a tempestuous season. The two chief reasons were: Don Newcombe was unbeatable for two months after his reinstatement from suspension for refusing to pitch batting practice; and Roy Campanella, his hand healed and strong, equaled his entire home-run output of 1954 in the first 54 games of 1955. Jackie Robinson hit well at the start, then tapered off to hover between .280 and .250, and a late-season slump left him with a final average of .256, his first under .300 since 1948. He failed to make the All-Star team, which didn't worry him, because he hadn't earned nomination. Besides, his Dodgers were pennant-bound. Nothing else mattered.

Brooklyn clinched the pennant in Milwaukee on September 8th, earliest in the League's 79-year history. They went into the World Series, underdogs, as usual, against the New York Yankees, facing them for the sixth time, and the fifth for Jackie. It was one of the most exciting of all, ending with a display of pitching courage by young Johnny Podres for his second victory and the big one. Duke Snider and Roy Campanella were the Dodgers' hitting heroes.

Jackie's batting slump found him on the bench for the seventh and last game, yet everyone who saw him in the opening contest at the Stadium conceded that his desire and daring had set the team "afire"—had demonstrated that you can manufacture a run without a base hit, just by taking advantage of breaks and using your legs and your heart and stealing home—even when you're close to 37 years of age.

On bare statistics, Jackie had one of his poorer Series, a .182 batting average and two errors at third base. But his team had won the World's Championship. Brooklyn had finally humbled the despised Yankees. And each Dodger player received $9,768.

"I've had my differences with Alston," Jackie said as the clubhouse bedlam subsided after the final game, "and even had my doubts about him, but I'll say this: Once we got rolling in the Series, he did a tremendous job, starting with that third game. He never got panicky. He held a couple of pep meetings and made some fine talks to the players. His confidence, I'm sure, rubbed off on the fellows and was a big factor in our comeback after losing those first two.

"Another thing: Campy was great and Duke got his ninth Series homer for a League record, but we never would've won without Pee Wee Reese. He was tremendous throughout the entire Series. To me he was the standout player. He made the big play and got the big hit whenever it meant something. It's a pleasure to be on the same team with him, and I hope I am next year. My wife would like to see me get in my tenth year. It's a great honor to be a ten-year man in the majors, and I'd sure like to become one."

Through the fall and early winter Jackie was busy with radio and television programs, and satisfying the endless demands for his presence at benefits and banquets. But he was not too busy to issue the usual number of veiled ultimatums about salary cut, and his unwillingness to be "cut to death." He had one brief encounter on salary with Vice-president Bavasi at the Montague Street office. His abrupt departure indicated a wide difference of opinion on the salary cut. Resulting headlines had him holding out through spring training, or quitting baseball, as he had so often threatened. And so it went into 1956.

On January 20th Jackie Robinson sat on a dais in Atlanta, Georgia, his native state, 225 miles north of his birthplace. Beside him sat Branch Rickey, who, at 74, had given up general management of the Pittsburgh Pirates, and was now board chairman and advisor to his youthful successor, Joe L. Brown. Both were honored guests of a large Negro fraternal and business gathering. During the dinner and the early part of the program they were able to talk at length for the first time in many years. Their chief topic was Jackie's baseball career and the inevitable end of it.

"A player of your ability," Rickey said at one point, "does not become useless overnight. You still have great value. True, it is a diminishing value, but if your good physical condition continues, you could have high value to any club for two, perhaps three more years.

"And remember, flattering business offers—even those made in the best of faith—have a way of disappearing when a great star loses his baseball identity. I have seen it happen too many times. Be cautious. Your career as a player may end, but I'm sure you have ambitions to manage, to be the first Negro manager in the major league. It may never happen, but your identity with baseball can still continue in some way, and it may well turn out to be the biggest financial asset of all."

Robinson then listened to this pioneering baseball man and benefactor receive a deafening ovation from the audience, not once, but three times during a stirring speech on "inter-racial progress within our country." Two nights later he heard this man cheered to the echo again at the Biltmore Hotel in New York. Branch Rickey had been invited to make the introduction of Jackie Robinson who was honored by the Sports Lodge of B'nai B'rith.

On the next day, Monday, January 23, Jackie made a "surprise" telephone call to Vice-president Bavasi at the Dodgers' office. He came to terms on salary quickly, and described his salary reduction to reporters as "no more than a hill of beans."

Now he would wear a Brooklyn Dodger uniform for the tenth straight year! And it turned out to be another pennant-winning year for Jackie's team with Jackie making a substantial contribution to that pennant. Atoning for his poor showing the previous year, he finished with a .275 average, ten home runs and 43 runs batted in—respectable for a "senior citizen" in baseball!

But as the season wore on, Robby just about wore out.

As the Dodgers prepared once more to face the Yankees in the World Series, Robinson was virtually swathed in adhesive and reeked of linament. Jack brought the Dodgers even in the sixth game of another Dodger-Yankee battle royal. His line drive over ancient Enos Slaughter's head accounted for the only run of the game as the Dodgers beat Bob Turley in ten innings. But the following day the Yanks took the Series.

Now, at the age of 38, after making a living playing baseball for twelve years, Robinson began once again to think he had had enough. It was time to consider his family and his future. Although he didn't know it then, in that final game of the 1956 World Series Robinson drew on his now famous number 42 for the last time.

For some time, Robinson's friend and agent, Martin Stone, had been looking out for the right kind of job. Then, early in December, 1956, William Black, president of the Chock Full O' Nuts restaurant chain, asked Robinson to work for him. The job sounded just right to Jack. The company had more than 1000 employees in the New York area, many of them Negro, and Jack was to be in charge of ironing out their problems and trying to keep personnel turnover to a minimum. After talking it over with his wife and family, Jack decided he would take the job.

But Robinson told no one else at this point. He had agreed some time before to give the story of his retirement from baseball to *Look Magazine* exclusively. Now that the day was at hand, he had to keep his word.

On the same day that Robinson signed up with his

new employer, the Dodger office informed him that he had been traded to the hated Giants for $30,000 and a left-handed journeyman pitcher. There had been rumors that Robby was on the trading block, but it was still a shock when Buzzie Bavasi told Robinson that he was to become a Giant. What Bavasi didn't know—in fact what nobody except Black, Robinson and his family knew—was that Robby had quit just a half hour before. He was not to become a Giant; he was to become an executive. But because of his strong sense of honor, he did not break his agreement with *Look*. It was not until January, 1957, when the *Look* story was released.

Because the working press had not been briefed first and because Robinson had not been getting along well with Bavasi and Walter O'Malley of the Dodgers, and because he had been traded to a rival team after a decade with the Dodgers, the sports pages burned with controversy for months.

Gradually the furor died down. Robinson settled happily into his new role and quickly proved to Black that he had more to offer than just his name. But Robinson continued to make news and he continued to fight for the principles he cherished.

Though Robinson had won many awards in his time, the greatest one was still to come.

The date was July 23, 1962. The place was Cooperstown, New York, a spot which organized baseball has sentimentally decided to call the "birthplace of the national pastime." The occasion was the induction of a new group of men into the most august body of those who ever played the sport from the very beginning. There he stood, this share-cropper baby from Cairo, Georgia, grandson of a freed slave, half-starved youth in Pasedena, California, a great collegiate athlete, soldier and officer in his country's army, batting champion of minor and major league baseball, Most Valuable Player in his League, the man who did it for his team when it had to be done, the man at the microphone before his Government—an individual voice personifying the urge of all men to be free to work and live as they wish. On this day of his first year of eligibility, Jack Roosevelt Robinson was formally voted into the Baseball Hall of Fame.

Standing just a few feet away while Robinson made his acceptance speech was his mentor, Branch Rickey, who smiled proudly as Robinson said: "Today everything is complete. I could not be here without the advice and guidance of three of the most wonderful people I know—my advisor, a wonderful friend and a man who has treated me as a father, Branch Rickey; my mother; and my wife. I never thought I'd make it in my lifetime."

What Robinson did not say that day was said by the learned Dr. Frank Tannenbaum in his masterpiece, *Slave and Citizen*, "Time—the long time—will draw a veil over the white and black of this hemisphere, and future generations will look back upon the record of strife as it stands revealed in the history of the people of this New World of ours with wonder and incredulity. For they will not understand the issues that the quarrel was about." [1]

[1] *Slave and Citizen* (Knopf), p. 129.

LIFETIME BATTING / FIELDING

Year	Team	G	AB	R	H	2B	3B	HR	TB	RBI	Avg.	PO	A	E	Avg.
1946	Montreal	124	444	113	155	25	8	3	205	66	.349	261	385	10	.985
1947	Brooklyn	151	590	125	175	31	5	12	252	48	.297	1323	92	16	.985
1948	Brooklyn	147	574	108	170	38	8	12	260	85	.296	514	342	15	.983
1949	Brooklyn	156	593	122	203	38	12	16	313	124	.342	395	421	16	.981
1950	Brooklyn	144	518	99	170	39	4	14	259	81	.328	359	390	11	.986
1951	Brooklyn	153	548	106	185	33	7	19	289	88	.338	390	435	7	.992
1952	Brooklyn	149	510	104	157	17	3	19	237	75	.308	353	400	20	.974
1953	Brooklyn	136	484	109	159	34	7	12	243	95	.329	238	126	6	.984
1954	Brooklyn	124	386	62	120	22	4	15	195	59	.311	166	109	7	.975
1955	Brooklyn	105	317	51	81	6	2	8	115	36	.256	100	183	10	.966
1956	Brooklyn	117	357	61	98	15	2	10	147	43	.275	169	230	9	.978
MAJOR LEAGUE TOTALS		1382	4877	947	1518	273	54	137	2310	734	.311	4007	2728	117	.983

WORLD SERIES

Year	Team	G	AB	R	H	2B	3B	HR	TB	RBI	Avg.	PO	A	E	Avg.
1947	Brooklyn	7	27	3	7	2	0	0	9	3	.259	49	6	0	1000
1949	Brooklyn	5	16	2	3	1	0	0	4	2	.188	12	9	1	.955
1952	Brooklyn	7	23	4	4	0	0	1	7	2	.174	10	20	0	1000
1953	Brooklyn	6	25	3	8	2	0	0	10	2	.320	8	0	0	1000
1955	Brooklyn	6	22	5	4	1	1	0	7	1	.182	4	18	2	.917
1956	Brooklyn	7	24	5	6	1	0	1	10	2	.250	5	12	0	1000
WORLD SERIES TOTALS		38	137	22	32	7	1	2	47	12	.234	88	65	3	.981

ALL-STAR GAMES

Year	Team	AB	R	H	2B	3B	HR	TB	RBI	Avg.	PO	A	E	Avg.
1949	Brooklyn	4	3	1	1	0	0	2	0	.250	1	1	0	1000
1950	Brooklyn	4	1	1	0	0	0	1	0	.250	3	2	0	1000
1951	Brooklyn	4	1	2	0	0	0	2	1	.500	3	1	1	.800
1952	Brooklyn	3	1	1	0	0	1	4	1	.333	2	2	0	1000
1953	Brooklyn	1	0	0	0	0	0	0	0	.000	0	0	0	.000
1954	Brooklyn	2	1	1	1	0	0	2	2	.500	0	0	0	.000
ALL-STAR GAME TOTALS (6 games)		18	7	6	2	0	1	11	4	.333	9	6	1	.938